Playing the Wife

A play

Ronald Hayman

Samuel French — London
New York - Toronto - Hollywood

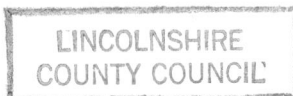

PLAYING THE WIFE

First presented at the Stranmillis Theatre, Belfast, on 25th
November 1992, with the following cast:

Strindberg	Barry Foster
Harriet	Julia Ormond
Bengt	Paul Spence
Gertrud	Jacqueline Morgan

Directed by Tim Pigott-Smith
Designed by Sue Willmington

Subsequently presented at the Minerva Theatre, Chichester,
on 13th July 1995, with the following cast:

Strindberg	Derek Jacobi
Harriet	Derbhle Crotty
Bengt	Jamie Glover
Gertrud	Caroline Holdaway

Directed by Richard Clifford
Décor by Julian McGowan

CHARACTERS

Strindberg is fifty-two but exceptionally young-looking, despite a slight puffiness in his face. Stocky, with a pinkish complexion. His fair wavy hair has lost its colour, but it's still thick, and he combs it upwards. He wears a bristly moustache and lets hair grow underneath his lower lip. Vanity is apparent in his posture and his way of moving.

Harriet is in her early twenties, with a slim, almost childish figure and long thick dark hair which is sometimes pinned up in a bun and sometimes hangs loose. With her big dark soulful eyes and her almost oriental features she could pass for a Javanese princess.

Bengt is in his middle or late twenties, fair, slim, tall, good-looking, working-class in origin but not in accent.

Gertrud is fortyish, spectacled, good-natured.

ACT I

SCENE 1

The stage and part of the auditorium in a late-19th century Stockholm theatre which has been damaged by fire

In the roof above the stage, not far from the centre, there is a hole. The charred flats of a set are still standing. It was built for a production at the turn of the century, and the back wall is almost intact. The set had a ceiling, which is badly burnt, but a blackened oil lamp still dangles on two of its three chains. US *are heaps of debris, including damaged furniture and singed carpets. Some* DS *space has been cleared for rehearsal, and seats have been removed from the front rows of the stalls. There is a table with various props on it — mentioned throughout the text — and a blonde wig on a wig-stand. The props are for the play which is being rehearsed, but at this stage the actual furniture for the play has not yet been bought. The actors use bits and pieces left in the theatre after the fire to rehearse with. There's an old writing table, salvaged from the abandoned set, and the only usable sofa has been singed by the fire. There are a few chairs scattered here and there, a gramophone and a lighting panel. In the stalls, close to the footlights, there is an armchair on one side and a lectern and a chair used by the stage manager on the other. There is a ladder* USC

Harriet enters, wearing a cloak, and a scarf over her head. It's snowing outside. She addresses the empty chair by the writing table

Harriet Listen to yourself. Listen to your voice — what you do to it. You try to unbalance yourself. (*She takes her cloak off and drapes it over the ladder*) Listen to yourself.

Gertrud enters, dressed as if she's been working for some time. She's carrying some papers

Listen to your voice — what you ——
Gertrud Morning.
Harriet — morning — (*still rehearsing her lines*) do to it. Why don't you post them yourself? ... Including this one? Do you really think I'm a lesbian? And a whore?

Bengt enters in outdoor clothes

Bengt Morning.
Gertrud Morning.
Bengt Would you like to run the scene?
Harriet Mmmm.

Bengt sits down at the writing table, still wearing his overcoat. Gertrud takes up her position at the lectern, ready to prompt. Harriet goes off to make another entrance, reading from a letter

"A cuckold in the theatre is a comic figure. I too would willingly laugh if someone else were the cuckold."
Bengt I knew you were stealing my letters.
Harriet Why don't you post them yourself?
Bengt I do — the ones I want to arrive. The ones I give you are the ones I want you to read.
Harriet Including this one? Do you really think I'm a lesbian? And a whore?
Bengt You want to have me locked up. That's what you want. In a madhouse.
Harriet I think you'd stopped loving me before we got married.
Bengt I still love you. But this is war, and we must fight to the end.
Gertrud (*prompting*) To the death.
Bengt Thanks ... We must fight to the death.
Harriet Do you really believe you aren't Karin's father?
Bengt Siri! Don't do this. You're playing with fire. Are you trying to drive me crazy?
Harriet You're crazy already if you think Karin isn't yours. Who do you think her father is?
Bengt Siri, I warn you. I can destroy you if I have to.
Harriet Listen to yourself. Listen to your voice — what you do to it. You deliberately unbalance yourself. When you were an actor, you failed, so you make marriage into a performance, testing, always testing how far you can go.
Bengt At least I know when to stop.
Harriet Not always.
Bengt Do I scare you?
Harriet Not as much as you scare yourself.
Bengt (*no longer acting*) Excuse me, Fröken Bosse, but I think you're forgetting what he said.
Harriet What?

Bengt He doesn't want you to engage the audience's sympathy.
Harriet I can't think about that when I'm inside a character.
Bengt He wants her to be more unsympathetic.
Harriet That's up to him. I'm not writing the dialogue.
Bengt But surely the way you said it ... I mean surely it's up to you whether Siri thinks she's in the right, or knows she's in the wrong.
Harriet She thinks she's in the right.
Bengt Not according to Herr Strindberg. And besides ...
Harriet What?
Bengt (*trying to take her hand*) Your hands are freezing. Put a coat on.
Harriet I can't work in the wrong clothes.
Bengt I think you're falling in love with her.
Harriet With Siri?
Bengt Just a bit.
Harriet Don't be ridiculous.

Strindberg enters, wearing a hat and a thick overcoat with a dusting of snow on them. He carries an attaché case

Gertrud is the first to see him

Gertrud Good-morning, Herr Strindberg!
Bengt Good-morning, Herr Strindberg.
Harriet Good-morning.
Strindberg Good-morning, Fröken Bosse, Herr Anders, Gertrud. I hope you aren't exhausted after yesterday. You started?
Bengt Just running the letter sequence.
Strindberg Good. We'll do some more work on it later. Gertrud, forgive me. I went away last night without thanking you for going out to fetch the wig.
Gertrud That's nothing, Herr Strindberg.
Strindberg Thank you. Herr Anders, please leave me alone with Fröken Bosse.
Bengt (*disconcerted*) Oh. Right. I'll be in my dressing-room.

He exits

Strindberg (*waiting for Bengt to go out of earshot*) It was wonderful. I couldn't believe it was happening. Could you?
Harriet I'm sorry?
Strindberg Women don't love. It's men who love and women who are loved. But when we were together last night, it was stupendous.
Harriet What?

Gertrud clears her throat

Strindberg Gertrud, get me a coffee. Very strong but some milk.

Gertrud exits

I knew immediately it was you but the first time I woke, I thought you were attacking me. I'd been reading Euripides, and there's a speech: "Do not let your heart be taken by an evil woman". But you said: "God bless you for the beautiful things you wrote about resurrection".

Harriet Are you talking about a dream?

Strindberg It started as a dream ...

Harriet I had a dream last night.

Strindberg I know. Mine would have been impossible if you weren't sharing it.

Harriet I dreamt about the rehearsal. Someone was saying: "Trust the voice".

Strindberg That's right. Don't impersonate Siri — *be* her. Trust your voice to *immerse* you.

Harriet But when I try to believe Bengt is you as you were then ...

Strindberg Think of him as a stranger who is also your husband. Make no effort. Your powers are greater than you realize. You've struck a note that has never been heard before. You'll be the actress of the new century if only you trust your voice, your dream, yourself.

Gertrud enters with a cup of coffee

Gertrud Do you want me to fetch Herr Anders?

Strindberg No. (*He consults his watch*) Yes. (*He takes his coat and hat off*)

Gertrud exits

It's freezing in here. (*He puts his hat and coat on again*) Where did you learn how to act?

Harriet My sister Alma taught me the most. She's eighteen years older than I am.

Strindberg Eighteen years older?

Harriet My parents had fourteen children. Seven are dead.

Strindberg You're Norwegian, aren't you?

Harriet I feel more Swedish than Norwegian. Herr Strindberg, could we leave this scene and work on something else?

Strindberg What do you want to do?

Harriet Could we go back to when Siri was married to the baron? I need more time on that period because I don't ...
Strindberg What?
Harriet You loved Siri but you never wanted to be alone with her.
Strindberg Don't try to understand intellectually. It's a matter of honour between men. You can't explain it to women. Except there's something I wrote last night ——

Bengt and Gertrud come back

(*To Gertrud*) Hand me my attaché case ... This is a new sequence. It comes near the beginning of the first act, after the boat scene. (*He takes out two copies of a manuscript, giving one to Harriet and Bengt and one to Gertrud*) Sit down. Just read.

Harriet and Bengt sit so that they can both read from the same script

(*To Gertrud*) Make copies of this. (*To Bengt*) Go ahead.
Bengt If you want me to go on visiting you, remember your duty to your husband. Jarl is a baron, but he's my friend. I love you to distraction but if you betray our secret by so much as a glance, I'll confess everything to him.
Harriet I wish I were as brave as you are. I should tell him everything.
Bengt If you do, I'll never see you again.
Harriet August!
Bengt What is there to tell him? We've done nothing wrong.
Harriet We haven't. He has. Do you know what happened last night when Tilda came?
Bengt Don't tell me. If he chooses to degrade himself with Tilda, that's his concern. What happens between us must be clean and beautiful and noble. We can talk about the love we feel for each other, but that's all.
Harriet Yes.
Strindberg That's not strong enough. You're full of admiration for me. Say, "That's wonderful".
Harriet That's wonderful.
Strindberg (*to Gertrud*) Change the line.

Bengt writes in the script

Go back.

The snow on the roof is melting. Water starts dripping on to the stage through the hole in the roof, a slow, regular drip. Strindberg looks up at the hole

Bengt We can talk about the love we feel for each other but that is all.
Harriet That's wonderful. And you'll always be faithful to me.
Strindberg Good.
Harriet I'm so excited, so happy. Of course, I'll never leave him. You know that. But you love me. Your secret is out, and I'm a guilty woman, because I love you in return. (*Praying*) Oh, God, forgive me for feeling so happy and calm. (*She stops acting*) She's not really calm, is she?
Strindberg No.
Harriet (*reading*) I love you with the tenderness of a sister, and I'll never ...
Gertrud Never forget my duties as a wife and mother.
Harriet I know the words. I've got a script.

Silence

Strindberg Take your time.

Silence

Is the noise distracting you? There's nothing we can do about it. The snow is melting. Spring will be here soon. If you concentrate hard enough, you won't hear it.
Harriet I can't play this part.
Strindberg Rehearsal conditions will be quite different once we get a theatre. We'll rehearse on the stage we're going to use.
Harriet I can't be Siri von Essen.
Strindberg You can play her. You're going to be good.
Harriet Just now you said "Be her".
Strindberg I was speaking to your imagination.
Harriet She's your wife.
Strindberg She's not my wife now, and she's no longer twenty-four.
Harriet You can't make her into a character.
Strindberg The only stories a man can tell are stories he's lived. She betrayed me.
Harriet If you want revenge, this is the wrong way to take it. It's between you and her — nothing to do with me.
Strindberg I think you'll find it is.

She stares at him and runs off

Bengt Shall I go and talk to her, Herr Strindberg?
Strindberg No. She'll come back. If the Powers want her to.
Bengt (*shyly*) May I ask you something?

Gertrud Herr Strindberg?
Strindberg Wait. I'm thinking. We've got to do something about that noise.
Gertrud There's a bucket in the props room. I could put it there to catch the
    drips.
Strindberg Go on then.
Gertrud Right. May I just ask you ...?
Strindberg What?
Gertrud I'm worried about leaving all these things in the theatre. I mean
    some of them are quite valuable, and anyone can get in any time.
Strindberg Are there no locks?
Gertrud The lock on the stage door still works but I can't even padlock the
    front entrance.
Strindberg Then lock the stage door and trust the Powers to keep watch on
    the front. All will be well. Fetch the bucket.

Gertrud exits

You had a question?
Bengt It's exciting to be you. To feel I'm impersonating, well, playing
    August Strindberg as you were thirty years ago ...
Strindberg Ask your question.
Bengt It's hard to bring your sympathetic ... the character's sympathetic and
    unsympathetic sides together.
Strindberg Stop trying.
Bengt Then I'd feel I was playing two different characters.
Strindberg Carry on like that as long as necessary and as soon as you can,
    increase it to three. Then four.
Bengt That's absolutely extraordinary.
Strindberg What is?
Bengt What you just said. As a young actor I sometimes feel ... May I say
    this? I think there's a corner to go round between being just competent and
    really good ... I may not have got round it yet but I know I have it in me
    to ... All I mean is ... Thank you. For what you said. It was helpful ...

He's still waiting for an answer when

Gertrud comes back with a bucket, which she tries to position

Strindberg Further that way.

She gets it into the right place but the noise is louder

You're making it worse.

Gertrud You prefer it without the bucket?

Strindberg I want the bucket but not the noise.

Bengt Excuse me, Herr Strindberg. I'm sorry it's not clean but I've only used it once. (*He takes out a handkerchief*) Maybe I should put it into the bucket myself. I mean so that Gertrud doesn't have to touch it. May I?

Strindberg Go on. Yes. Go on.

Bengt sacrifices his handkerchief

Gertrud I'll wash it for you afterwards.

Bengt Thanks, Gertrud.

Strindberg We're wasting so much time. Set up the scene on the boat. We'll do some work on that.

Gertrud Certainly, Herr Strindberg.

From the pile of props and junk at the side of the stage she lifts four short vertical posts joined together with a rope. They're too heavy for her

Strindberg Give her a hand.

Bengt helps her to position them so that they represent the edge of a ship's deck

Strindberg Don't forget the lantern.

Gertrud No, Herr Strindberg.

She hangs a lantern on the deck and sets it swinging

I'm ready, Herr Strindberg. Shall I call Fröken Bosse?

Strindberg No, don't call her.

Bengt She said she didn't want to play Siri. Do you think she's going to be all right?

Strindberg Of course.

Bengt Shall I go and have a word with her?

Strindberg No. She'll come when we're ready for her. (*Facing towards the dressing-room, he braces himself, legs apart, knees tight, arms open, as if trying to communicate with her telepathically*)

Gertrud But we are ready, Herr Strindberg.

Strindberg Then she'll come. Give Herr Anders his walking-stick.

Gertrud gives Bengt a walking-stick and he puts on his overcoat and hat. Pacing about the deck, he twirls the stick. The prolonged silence becomes awkward as Strindberg exerts more telepathic effort

Bengt You wouldn't like me ——
Strindberg Wait.

Another awkward silence

Harriet appears

We're going to do the scene on the boat. You'll be all right. Don't say anything. Just do it. Give her the parasol.

Gertrud gives Harriet a parasol and Bengt offers his arm. They go into the scene, which they know well enough to rehearse without scripts. Harriet wears a hat with a veil

Harriet August, this is the first time we've been alone together.
Bengt I know. Because your husband always ——
Harriet No, it was you. Jarl wanted you to escort me so he could be with Tilda but you made some excuse. You're always making excuses.
Bengt Whatever you say, Baroness.
Harriet (*moving away*) We were on a boat when he first said he loved me. Just as he spoke, a shooting-star made a brilliant arc across the sky.
Strindberg Stop it! Stop! Don't look at her like that. Don't devour her. What you want is to worship her.
Bengt Yes, I see that, but ——
Strindberg You've lost your faith. This is the woman who can fill the void. You're yearning for a virgin mother to adore. She looked so pure when her children were with her, I could almost believe in immaculate conception.
Bengt Should I feel no desire?
Strindberg You want to be her guardian angel. You'd die to protect her. It's partly your lower-class instincts. You respect pure blood, a superior race.
Bengt I hadn't understood that.
Strindberg (*going towards his chair*) I know.
Bengt Shall I go back?
Strindberg No, go from the shooting-star. But don't look sexually hungry.
Harriet A shooting-star made a brilliant arc across the sky. He was always good to me then but now he's annoyed he hasn't got a whole weekend with Tilda.
Bengt My dear Baroness, if you need to complain about your husband, please do so in his presence.
Harriet How dare you? You're insulting me.
Bengt Yes, my dear Baroness. I'm insulting you.

Harriet (*to Strindberg*) Is that really what you said?

Strindberg I may not have used those words. Go on. This is where you see the crack in the statute of the Virgin. The beautiful aristocrat is just an animal, treacherous, dangerous, ready to pounce on me with sharp claws if I side with the husband she's ready to betray.

Harriet I'm not betraying him, he's betraying me.

Strindberg In love-affairs the man is never the betrayer.

Harriet Jarl's been taking advantage of my absence.

Strindberg Jarl's been taking what Jarl's been given. Carry on.

Harriet I don't think you like women.

Strindberg Look at the facts. The virgin sells herself as a bride to the highest bidder. The unfaithful wife gives her lover what belongs to her husband.

Harriet (*trying to adjust her veil*) No.

Bengt Excuse me, but arguments aren't going to help.

Harriet From Siri's point of view ——

Bengt What interests me is the way they both shift their position.

Strindberg Of course they do.

Bengt Can't we concentrate on that? I find it hard to line up this bit with the next bit, when Siri says she's *not* jealous.

He crosses to look at Gertrud's script. Harriet is still fiddling with her veil

Strindberg Come here. I can't see your face. If you ... (*he adjusts it for her*) What are you doing? (*He recoils*)

Harriet What do you mean?

Strindberg We won't speak about it.

Harriet What did I do?

Strindberg You're incredible. Let's not discuss it. (*Making an effort to control himself, he gives her a wide berth*) Go on with the scene. Go on.

Bengt Yes, my dear Baroness. I'm insulting you.

Harriet I'm not ready. Give me that line again.

Strindberg Yes, my dear Baroness. I'm insulting you.

Harriet I'm cold. I'm terribly cold.

Strindberg Gertrud, see if there's a stove.

Gertrud exits

Bengt I know something's troubling you. If I can be of the slightest help, please make use of my friendship.

Harriet It's my fault that Jarl's having difficulties. My dowry was in shares that turned out to be worthless.

Bengt Better times are coming. The stockmarket will improve.

Harriet I've dried.

Strindberg Gertrud!
Gertrud (*off*) Coming.
Strindberg Can't you stay on the book? (*He goes to her script*)

Gertrud enters

Gertrud You sent me to look for a stove.
Strindberg That will be too late.
Gertrud Don't you want it now?
Strindberg Of course I want it. The line is "That will be too late".
Harriet That will be too late. I must do something to help him ... I'm sorry.

Bengt takes off his jacket and offers it to Harriet but she doesn't take it

Strindberg We'll do something else. I'll work with Fröken Bosse on her own.
Bengt You don't need me?
Strindberg No.
Bengt Right. I'll be in my ... I'll see you later.

He does his best to make a dignified exit

Strindberg Gertrud, make us something hot to drink.
Gertrud Tea or coffee?
Strindberg Either.

Gertrud exits

Take that off. You look like Siri.

She takes the hat off

Why did you do that?
Harriet What?
Strindberg You know what you did
Harriet You mean the way I was playing the scene?
Strindberg No.
Harriet I don't understand.
Strindberg I think there are two of you.
Harriet What do you mean?
Strindberg One of you pretends there's nothing going on. I'll speak to the other one. (*Addressing an invisible woman on the other side of the stage*) I knew it would happen but I wasn't expecting it so soon.

Harriet What are you doing?

Strindberg You should take her into your confidence. Tell her that when I adjusted her veil, her face grew larger and more beautiful. Her eyes stabbed me with flashes of black lightning, and her lips moved against mine. She was in my room all night. We're going to be married.

Harriet You're asking too much of me.

Strindberg "Behold the man who summoned me," she said. Gave me her naked foot to kiss.

Harriet You mustn't do this.

Strindberg (*to the real Harriet*) You had no breasts. Nothing at all. The snow is still thick on the ground but the sun has begun to shine.

Harriet You mustn't do this.

Strindberg I'll buy roses for you. With thorns, of course.

Harriet (*not wholly displeased*) I'm not listening.

Strindberg (*looking upwards, kneeling to pray*) Give us a sign of your will. Fröken Bosse will obey.

Harriet (*glancing upwards*) I will not.

Strindberg You believe things happen by chance?

Harriet No.

Strindberg I saw a notice outside a house in Karlavägen. "Flats available." Siri and I lived there.

Harriet What are you saying?

Strindberg A band was playing a festive march out on the ice. You don't think the Powers are teasing us?

Harriet Do you?

Strindberg What were you doing at nine o'clock yesterday evening? You were reading something I'd written, but not a play.

Harriet How do you know that?

Strindberg Stop haunting me. When you do, I can't escape. By eleven it was so intense I had to possess you.

Gertrud enters with tea

Not now. I don't want a tea-break now. Never make tea unless I tell you.

Gertrud You did tell me.

Strindberg Don't argue with me. Who do you think you are?

Harriet You did tell her.

Strindberg Did I? I'm sorry, Gertrud. Please forgive me. I shouldn't have shouted. I do remember asking you. Of course I do. It went out of my mind. Thank you. Would you like a cup of tea, Fröken Bosse?

Harriet shakes her head

I'll have some. (*To Gertrud*) Have the other cup yourself. Gertrud!

Gertrud What is it, Herr Strindberg?
Strindberg Take your glasses off.

She does so

My favourite shade of blue. Now fetch Herr Anders, would you? We'll do
the scene where you want me to come and live in your house.

Gertrud exits

It would of course be improper if I invited you to my rooms. But if I tell you
the table will be laid for supper at seven-thirty, you can decide whether to
honour me with another visit.

Harriet is speechless

Please yourself. The table will be cleared at eight.
Harriet Aren't you going to the Dramatenteater?
Strindberg I never go to first nights, not even other people's.
Harriet When a play of yours is coming to life for the first time in front of
an audience ...
Strindberg The excitement will be present in my room. I'd like you to share
it. Will you?

Gertrud comes back

Gertrud He's not there.
Strindberg Who's not there?
Gertrud Herr Anders. Not in his dressing-room.
Strindberg Then where is he?
Gertrud I don't know.
Strindberg Find him.
Gertrud I've looked. I've a feeling he's not in the theatre.
Strindberg Of course he's in the theatre. He's an actor. Actors don't leave
the theatre until they're dismissed. Look for him.
Gertrud I've looked.
Strindberg Look again. Look harder.

Gertrud exits

Fröken Bosse.
Harriet Yes.

Strindberg (*going to his attaché case*) Would you do something for me?
Harriet What?
Strindberg You have an instinct for truth. I'd like you to read my new play. It's not finished, but there's a part for you.

He offers her a script. She can't speak but she accepts it

Bengt comes in, holding a parcel. There is snow on his jacket

Strindberg Where were you? I needed you.
Bengt I'm sorry. I had to go out.
Harriet You're shivering.
Bengt I rushed out without an overcoat. This is for you.
Harriet For me?
Bengt It's nothing. Just because you're cold. It's nothing.

She opens the parcel and takes out a shawl

Harriet You bought it? You shouldn't have.
Bengt You were cold.
Harriet Thank you. You're very kind. (*She offers her hand*)
Bengt (*shaking it*) The pleasure is mine. Please wear it. I mean it's yours. Do whatever you want with it. Obviously.
Harriet (*putting it on*) Thank you. It feels good.
Bengt It's the warmest they had in the shop.
Harriet You're very kind.
Bengt It's nothing.
Strindberg (*discomfited*) So you keep saying, but we must work. The scene when you tell him about the room in your house. Gertrud! Where's Gertrud? She went to look for you. You should have been here. Gertrud!

Strindberg exits

Harriet Herr Anders, you must help me. Please. Never leave me alone with him.
Bengt What happened?
Harriet Nothing. Don't ever leave me with him.
Bengt What if he sends me off stage?
Harriet Go into the stalls and make sure he knows you're there. He's mad. He may be a great writer but he's mad.
Bengt You're sure it's not an act he puts on?
Harriet He thinks I've been to his rooms. I don't even know where they are but he talks as if we've ...

Act I, Scene 1

Bengt You mean ...
Harriet Yes.
Bengt That *is* mad.
Harriet And he talked as if there were two of me. He spoke to the other one.
  She was over there. But he said what he wanted me to hear.
Bengt That's the trick he uses in the play. Giving her letters to post when he
  wants her to read them.
Harriet Help me.
Bengt You must leave Stockholm.
Harriet What about the play?
Bengt I know. I know.
Harriet It's the best part I've ever had.
Bengt Mine's the best I've had but we still don't know when we're supposed
  to open. Or *where*.
Harriet I know. Why are we doing this?
Bengt These rehearsals are pointless. He says we'll work in the new theatre
  as soon as we know where ...
Harriet Shh!

Strindberg comes back in with Gertrud

Strindberg Come on. We must get on. Siri comes to his rooms.
Harriet What?
Strindberg You come to his rooms and find him in bed, ill. Gertrud.

*As Gertrud starts to set up, Harriet adjusts her costume and Bengt looks at
his script*

Harriet Is this the first time I've been to his rooms?
Strindberg No, you've been before. You know that.
Harriet I get confused when ... when we do scenes out of order.
Strindberg It's the best way to rehearse, and the best way to write. Things
  seems to happen in order, but it's only chronological. You'll get used to my
  way of working.
Gertrud (*moving the sofa into position*) Is that right?
Strindberg Further downstage.

Bengt helps her to move it

Further to the right.

They reposition it

More at an angle.

They move it again

Begin.

Bengt lies down. Gertrud puts a decanter and a glass by the sofa. Harriet makes her entrance and wakes Bengt up by blowing gently in his ear

Bengt It's not really you. I'm dreaming.
Harriet You're not dreaming. I'm here. My poor boy. (*She puts her hand to his brow*) Jarl's coming. He has news for you.
Bengt What news?
Harriet He'll tell you. Do you have a thermometer?
Bengt I'd like a drink of water.

Harriet pours water for Bengt

   Is this drinking water, Gertrud?
Gertrud No, I don't think ——
Strindberg Yes, yes, drink it. Go on. You won't die.
Bengt (*drinking*) What's the news?
Harriet Good news. We'll be able to see more of you. He's going to give you a room in our house.
Bengt I shan't accept.
Harriet You must accept.
Strindberg More imperious. Be strong when he's weak and moody when he asserts himself.
Bengt I shan't accept.
Harriet You must accept. It's not for your sake. It'll be nicer for us.
Bengt My dear Baroness, what would people say if you took a bachelor into your home?
Harriet Who cares what they say?
Bengt What about your mother? No, a man can't allow himself ——
Harriet A man can't live in a poky little attic.
Bengt The one thing a man must do is show himself to be strong.
Strindberg Stop. Fröken Bosse, the sincerity and motherly tenderness are all right but she's also flirtatious, charmingly provocative. I'll tell you one of her tricks. She had a way of dropping her head towards me. It was aristocratic and seductive at the same time. She has her sulky silences, but women are conscious of being looked at when they expose their ankles. Search for moments when you can flirt with your ankles. Carry on.

Bengt My dear Baroness, what would people say if you took a bachelor into your home?
Harriet (*subtly flirtatious*) Who cares what they say?
Strindberg Wait. I have to ... wash my hands.

He exits

Bengt Well, really! Do we go on or do we wait?
Gertrud He won't be long.
Bengt How do you know?
Gertrud If he goes to wash his hands, it's only a minute or two, but if he needs to lie down, it can be a long wait. When he comes back, he carries on as if nothing's happened.

She exits

Bengt He can't expect us to keep switching on and off. What does he think we are? Let's go on. (*He lies down again*)
Harriet I don't want to.
Bengt You want to sit and wait?
Harriet No.
Bengt So what do you want to do?
Harriet Nothing.
Bengt We could run the lines at least.
Harriet Leave me alone. Please. Just don't talk. I don't want to rehearse and I don't want to chatter.
Bengt Until he gets back. Then your mood will suddenly change.
Harriet If it does, it does.
Bengt Right.

Silence. She moves about, Bengt takes his cigarettes out

Gertrud returns with a stove

Harriet Give me a cigarette.
Bengt You don't smoke.
Harriet I'm going to start.
Bengt Is that wise?
Harriet Give me a cigarette.

He does. He gropes in his pockets

Bengt I've run out of matches.
Harriet Oh, really!
Gertrud I'll get some.

She exits

Harriet I hate this place.
Bengt It's just a theatre. Slightly wounded. A wounded theatre.
Harriet I hate theatres. They're drab and smelly.
Bengt It's the damp.
Harriet It's stupid having a bucket to catch the drips. (*She kicks the bucket across the stage*) I hate being an actress. You sit around waiting for something to happen, and when it does, it's always disappointing.
Bengt I've never seen you like this.
Harriet You don't know me.
Bengt Have dinner with me tonight.
Harriet I can't. (*Touching the shawl*) But thank you for this.

Silence

Bengt Do you think his enemies did it?
Harriet What?
Bengt Started the fire.
Harriet No idea. He doesn't suffer from any shortage.
Bengt What?
Harriet He has plenty of enemies.
Bengt But you don't really think it's them ... I mean it's not his theatre, and it wasn't a play of his that was on when it caught fire.
Harriet I know.

Silence

Bengt I've never done this before. It's weird.
Harriet What is?
Bengt Rehearsing without knowing where we're going to open.
Harriet Why is she taking so long to find matches?
Bengt I expect they were all used up by the person who started the fire.
Harriet I hate this place. It's cold and damp, and it smells of defeat. I thought rehearsing with Strindberg would be wonderful. But I can't work like this. I feel naked, prostituted. What if she comes to one of the performances?
Bengt Who?
Harriet Siri von Essen.

Bengt You should hear the way you say her name. She won't come. She's in Finland.

Harriet She might read about it in the papers. What if she came round after the play and said, "I'm Siri von Essen"? (*She shudders*) If someone told me she was in the audience, I couldn't go on.

Bengt She won't come.

Harriet You don't know.

Bengt Don't think about it.

Harriet I wouldn't mind if it was really her. It's his version of her.

Gertrud enters with matches

Gertrud He's coming back. Sorry I was so long. (*She gives the matches to Bengt*)

Bengt Thanks, Gertrud

Strindberg enters with wet hands

Strindberg Why is there no towel in the cloakroom?

Gertrud I've got one for you, Herr Strindberg.

Strindberg We're wasting so much time. We'll do a scene towards the end. The collapse. (*To Bengt*) Your pen is still in your hand.

Gertrud hands him a towel

Strindberg What's this for? Oh. (*He dries his hands*) And try for *once* to play the scene through without stopping. We'll never get the rhythms right till we've got more momentum.

He climbs down into the stalls. Bengt clutches his throat and collapses. Harriet looks glad, thinking he's dead, but when she stoops over him, she sees he isn't and loosens his tie

Harriet Are you all right?

Bengt It's the end.

Harriet No!

Bengt Not scared of dying. More than death to scare me.

Harriet I'll call a doctor.

Bengt No.

Harriet Why not?

Bengt Want to die. Too disgusting. Sick of fighting.

Harriet You can't leave us in a foreign country with no money. How can we get home?

Bengt Life insurance. You back.
Harriet But you can't just lie there.
Strindberg (*from the stalls*) Register a change. Now you know there's insurance money, you're less anxious.
Harriet How can we get home?
Bengt Life insurance. You back.
Harriet But you can't just lie there. I'll put a cushion under your head.
Bengt Uh.
Harriet Better?
Bengt Bit.
Harriet (*putting her hand on his brow*) You're cold. (*She strokes his forehead*)
Bengt Better. Evil spirits going.
Harriet Am I driving them out? Could you eat? I've made some broth. It would do you good.
Strindberg Stop. (*He climbs up on stage*) It's too restrained, too old-fashioned. You weren't bad, Harriet. But (*to Bengt*) you're still trying to be a character. People aren't characters. We're inconsistent, out of joint.
Bengt Excuse me, Herr Strindberg, he is a character.
Strindberg You'll never be any good till you learn not to think like that. Am I always consistent? Is there a clear-cut outline all round me? Or her? Or you? Nothing about us is static. We're improper fractions, top-heavy, ramshackle assemblages from scraps of feeling and thought. Sometimes we do things, and if there's a reason for them, we have no idea what it is. I'll show you. I shouldn't. The doctor says I mustn't exert myself, but who cares? Give me music.
Gertrud Excuse me. Herr Strindberg, but if the doctor says ——
Strindberg Music.
Gertrud What music would you like?
Strindberg "The Entry of the Boyars". Piano version. Anything, but don't make me wait. Quick. (*To Bengt*) If you should ever play the Captain in *The Dance of Death*, don't think of him as me. He's a refined demon. Evil shines out of his eyes — glints of Satanic humour. Come on, Gertrud. When he says those evil things, he licks his fat lips, rolls the malice around on his tongue, relishing the taste.

Gertrud, who has found a record, winds up the gramophone

Gertrud! Quick! He thinks he's clever, but like all bullies he's a coward. And as soon as the music starts ...

Piano music. Saint-Saëns' "Danse Macabre"

Gertrud.

Gertrud Yes, Herr Strindberg.

Strindberg Thank you for you profound and sympathetic understanding of the way momentum in the theatre has to be built up and sustained. (*To the others*) After twenty years of marriage, she still thinks she can pacify me by playing the piano. (*He starts stamping to the rhythm*) The dance is furious, because there's lots of life in him and he can't use it. (*Now he's dancing*) Anger is the creative force, and the hardest to master. This is a death-dance. To get the full flavour of the human, go beyond the human. The truth about life is monstrous. Monstrous. (*He bellows with rage and pain. Out of breath, he makes his way back to the chair*)

Bengt Are you all right?

Strindberg nods, but, sitting in the chair, he clutches his heart and falls back, sprawling motionless. The music has stopped and the needle is scratching in the groove

Gertrud (*screaming*) Help him!
Bengt Oh my God!
Gertrud (*trying to revive him*) Help me.

Strindberg is laughing

Thank God. (*She crosses herself*)

Harriet is the only one who hasn't panicked

Strindberg A good actress isn't easily fooled. Stop that machine.

Gertrud stops the record

(*He gets up. To Bengt*) I hope you learned something.
Bengt But Herr Strindberg, how does that apply to my collapse in the play?
Strindberg You must make it more real than reality, but maliciously deceptive, totally false. You want to be a good actor? Stop being a good boy. Liberate the malice inside you.
Bengt Please don't patronize me, Herr Strindberg.
Strindberg I'm trying to help you. You want help? You need it.
Harriet Don't patronize him.
Strindberg (*angrily*) Don't be so — (*he checks himself*) quick to judge me. Cut to where she brings in the soup.

Bengt lies down. Harriet fetches a tureen and a bowl from the prop table

Harriet How are you feeling?
Bengt (*staring through the window*) Look.
Harriet What?
Bengt The green of the vines. The scarlet on the quince tree. Listen.
Harriet What?
Bengt Cowbells in the distance.
Harriet Just a moment.

Silence

Bengt What is it?
Harriet Hush!

Silence

I thought I could hear a bird.
Bengt I can't hear anything.
Harriet I think a bird has flown into the theatre. Do you think it will find its way out?
Strindberg Go on with the scene.
Bengt Cowbells in the distance.
Harriet (*offering him a bowl of broth*) Drink it while it's hot.

Pause. He doesn't drink any

Bengt I haven't got long to live. There's something I must tell you.
Harriet Drink it.
Bengt I sacrificed your career as an actress for mine as a writer. Can you forgive me?
Harriet Of course. Drink your broth.
Bengt Promise you'll go back on the stage.
Harriet Do I have to drink a spoonful to prove it's not poisoned?
Bengt No. (*He mimes drinking from the bowl*)
Harriet You aren't dying. You feel drowsy?
Bengt (*as if sleepy*) I forgive you for everything, even this.
Harriet May I suggest something? Why don't I feed him, like a mother with a child?
Strindberg No, he still thinks she's poisoning him.
Harriet I know that.
Strindberg It's better the way it is.
Harriet Why shouldn't she feed him poison in spoonfuls?

Strindberg It's not poisoned.
Harriet I know it's not, but ——
Strindberg Let's stick to what I've written, shall we?

In the silence, melted ice starts dripping into the space where the bucket was

(*To Gertrud*) I told you to put a bucket there.
Gertrud I did put a bucket there.
Strindberg I can't see it.
Gertrud Perhaps it got moved.
Strindberg It couldn't get moved unless someone moved it. Why would anyone move it!
Gertrud I don't know.
Harriet I moved it.
Strindberg You moved the bucket?
Harriet Yes.
Strindberg Why?
Harriet (*more submissive than defiant*) Sometimes we do things, and if there's a reason for them, we have no idea what it is.

Silence

Strindberg Where did you put it?
Harriet I don't know.
Strindberg You must know where you put it. Gertrud, look for it.

Gertrud starts to look

Bengt (*picking it up*) It's over here.

He puts it in position

Strindberg Now can we please get on with the scene?
Bengt (*lying down, as before*) I forgive you for everything, even this.

The handkerchief has fallen out of the bucket, and water patters loudly on the metal

Strindberg Where's the handkerchief?
Bengt I don't know.
Gertrud I'll get a cloth. (*She silences the bucket with a cloth*)
Strindberg We must get more work done. Gertrud, the dog scene.

Harriet The dog scene? We can't do the dog scene now.

Gertrud waits

Strindberg Why not?
Harriet It doesn't come till after they're married. How can we get our minds
around to that when we've just ——
Strindberg Because that's what life is like. You never know what's going
to come next. The dog scene.

Gertrud starts rearranging the chairs

Harriet I haven't looked at it for days. I'll have to use my script.
Strindberg Try it without. Gertrud will prompt you.

*While Harriet looks at a script, Gertrud positions two chairs on either side
of a table*

Ready?
Gertrud Wait a minute. (*She arranges some crockery and cutlery*) Right.

*Harriet and Bengt sit down at the table. They mime eating soup. Gertrud
yelps like a dog*

Harriet Poor Waffles!
Bengt This is torture.
Harriet He'd be quiet if only he could come in.
Bengt He's not coming in here while I'm eating.
Harriet I'm sure he'd be good.
Bengt The subject is closed.
Harriet All right.

More yelping from Gertrud

Bengt Be quiet!

Louder yelping

Are we going to have this every mealtime?
Harriet What can I do?
Bengt Rat poison?
Harriet Gusten!

Bengt You know I hate dogs. I always have. Their function is to protect cowards without the courage to fight an assailant.
Harriet What about old women?
Bengt What about them?
Harriet They can't fight assailants.
Bengt You're not an old woman, and you have me to protect you. You should have asked me before you offered to take him.
Harriet I couldn't leave him with Jarl. Jarl was cruel to him.
Bengt Not as cruel as I'm going to be.

More yelping

Quiet!
Harriet Let him come in. Just for this evening.
Bengt No.
Harriet Please. I promise not to feed him at table.
Bengt That's what you said last time.
Harriet I forgot. Just once.
Bengt It's unhygienic. His spittle gets on your fingers. Which go to your mouth. You swallow dog spittle. Anyway, he reminds me of your life with Jarl.
Harriet You're not really jealous. You're pretending. You don't love me any more.
Bengt I love you, but I hate your dog.
Harriet If you love me, you must love Waffles.
Bengt (*seeing something on the floor*) What's that?
Harriet What?
Bengt There.
Harriet Nothing. (*She gets up*) I'll clean it up.
Bengt Stay where you are. (*He gets up. As himself*) Which door is it?
Gertrud This one.
Bengt (*opening the door*) The dog isn't here.
Gertrud Sorry.

She hands him a mop-head. She whimpers and yelps as he grabs it by what's meant to be the scruff of its neck. He marches across to the dog shit and rubs the dog's nose in it. A crescendo of yelping

Harriet Gusten.
Bengt He has to be punished.
Harriet (*getting up*) Don't hurt him. I can't bear it.

Gertrud keeps up the yelping and whimpering

Bengt If you do that again, I'll kill you.
Harriet Gusten!
Bengt You filthy beast! (*He marches back to the door, throws the dog inside and mimes shutting it*)
Harriet Poor Waffles!
Gertrud Curtain!

Harriet and Bengt wait for Strindberg's reactions

Strindberg It's not working. It's unbalanced.
Bengt I thought it was quite good.
Strindberg (*to Harriet*) The point about the dog is you associate it with Marta.
Harriet Marta?
Strindberg Your daughter. Marta. She died when she was three. Waffles was her dog.
Harriet You never told me that.
Strindberg I'm telling you now.
Harriet There's nothing about Marta in the script.
Strindberg Her only relevance is her effect on your attitude to Waffles.
Harriet That's exactly what a man would say. That's why the scene is unbalanced. How is the audience supposed to see why I love Waffles?
Strindberg It's the quality of your love that matters ...
Harriet Marta makes a difference. I need a line about her.
Strindberg I'll think about it. Gertrud, set up the scene where Jarl gives us permission to see each other.
Bengt Can we break for five minutes?
Strindberg No. Help Gertrud.

Bengt helps Gertrud shift the furniture. Harriet helps too

Are you ready? We must keep up the momentum. I want the energy from one scene to carry forward into the next.
Harriet But this comes earlier.
Strindberg Which means they're fresher. You can't control your input of energy till you've had practice in moving backwards and forwards. I need you to be more athletic. Are you ready?
Gertrud Yes, Herr Strindberg.
Strindberg Then take up your positions for the start of the sequence.

Harriet and Bengt do so

Gertrud Lights about to change. Lights change.

Harriet enters

Harriet Good news.
Bengt What is it?
Harriet It's going to be all right. I've told him everything.
Bengt Jarl?
Harriet Yes.
Bengt Everything?
Harriet Yes.
Bengt You should have discussed it with me first.
Harriet You know what he did? Guess?

Silence

I don't know whether he's a great baby, or a cunning fox. He wept. Big, hot
tears. He loves both of us. You can still come to the house, but we have to
go on as we are.
Bengt What does that mean?
Harriet Like brother and sister. We can kiss and cuddle, but no inchastity.
Bengt Huh!
Harriet I'm so relieved it's out in the open. Now we don't have to feel
ashamed.
Bengt Let's never see each other again.
Harriet What?
Bengt You think I'd agree to that?
Harriet To what? Nothing's different.
Bengt He's insulting my manhood, and so are you.
Harriet It's exactly what you said we should do.
Bengt It's different if I say it. If Jarl thinks he can control what we do, we'll
never see each other again.
Harriet Ah. (*She collapses in a faked faint*)
Strindberg No. Stop.

She gets up

You're forgetting Siri had no talent as an actress. That was too lifelike.

Harriet faints less convincingly

That's better.

Bengt Was that good enough to take me in?
Strindberg Quite good enough. You're too besotted to be suspicious.

Bengt tries to revive her. He pours a glass of water, but fails to make her drink it

Darling.
Harriet (*faintly*) Where am I?
Bengt Are you all right?
Harriet What happened?
Bengt See if you can stand up.

She tries, falls back. He tries to pick her up. Fails. She moves into an easier position. He lifts her and carries her to the couch

Harriet I need a doctor. Where are you going?
Bengt To fetch a doctor.
Harriet Don't leave me.
Bengt I don't want to.
Harriet What is it?
Bengt You're so beautiful.
Harriet There are tears in your eyes.
Bengt I love you so much.
Harriet Now I've seen you both cry on the same day.
Bengt I'm too happy, that's the trouble.

He kneels at her feet and kisses her boots. Some of the black polish comes off on his lips

Harriet Come here.
Bengt Oh, I love you.

He lies down next to her and they kiss

I can love you chastely. I can.
Strindberg Stop. You've both got black lips.
Bengt Wouldn't it be good to bring some comedy into it?
Strindberg The balance has to be right.

Gertrud gives Bengt a towel

We need dignity here. Jarl is the aristocracy on the way down. I'm the servant class on the way up. Siri doesn't know that mentally, but she does physically. Show it with your body. It was a mistake to have a child with Jarl. When you embrace me on the couch, you want children from a commoner. That's how to survive. I'm the future. Go on.

Harriet embraces Bengt passionately

Strindberg I must go and wash.

He exits

Bengt Gertrud, be an angel. I'm terribly thirsty.
Gertrud Coffee?
Bengt That would be marvellous.
Gertrud Right.

She exits

Bengt Have dinner with me tonight. Please say yes.
Harriet I can't.
Bengt You can. We have to talk. Why can't you?
Harriet He wants to go over some lines with me.
Bengt Where?
Harriet In his rooms.
Bengt Do you know what you're doing?
Harriet I'll be all right.
Bengt You said you never wanted to be alone with him.
Harriet I was being silly. I felt scared.
Bengt Anything could happen.
Harriet No.
Bengt Either he's mad or he's playing the madman to get his own way.
Harriet I'll be all right.
Bengt If he gets you alone ...
Harriet The landlady will be there. Let's do some work.
Bengt You mustn't go there tonight. I have a reason.
Harriet What reason?
Bengt I can't tell you. I made a promise. Didn't you?
Harriet What promise?
Bengt Not to read his novels.
Harriet Yes. One of them tells the same story as this play.
Bengt There are things in that novel he doesn't want us to know. You're in danger, Fröken Bosse. You know how old he is?

Harriet No.
Bengt Guess.
Harriet I can never tell with men. Late forties?
Bengt Fifty-two, and he still thinks he's the future. That's what he said. He says he's working-class, but he isn't. Not really. His mother was a maid, but his father claimed to be descended from the aristocracy.
Harriet And you? Are you pure working-class?
Bengt I am actually.
Harriet You don't sound it.
Bengt I did till I went to theatre school. Don't go to his rooms. Please.
Harriet Have you read the novel?
Bengt Yes.
Harriet After promising not to?
Bengt No. Before. He didn't ask whether I'd read it, just made me promise not to. If you'd read it, you wouldn't have anything to do with him.
Harriet Why?

Bengt makes a gesture of frustration

Is it a matter of honour between men? Something women can't understand?
Bengt Not at all.
Harriet You don't know much about women, do you? You're trying to stop me going, but you're arousing my curiosity.
Bengt Let's do some work. Let's go on from where we stopped. ... I'm too happy. That's the trouble.
Harriet Come here.
Bengt Oh, I love you.

He lies down next to her and they kiss

I can love you chastely. I can. But it has nothing to do with him. It's because of us, what we want. No other man imposes conditions on me.
Harriet (*not acting*) May I say something?
Bengt Of course.
Harriet This isn't Strindberg as he is now. This is a young man who doesn't know where he's going.
Bengt Am I overdoing the male pride?
Harriet Yes.

Gertrud enters

Bengt Let's go back. ... I'm too happy. That's the trouble.
Harriet Come here. Lie beside me.
Bengt Oh, I love you.

He lies down. The kiss goes on longer than it did before

Strindberg enters

Gertrud (*prompting to alert them to his presence*) I can love you chastely.
Bengt I can love you chastely. (*He sees Strindberg*)

Fade to Black-out

SCENE 2

The ladder has been moved DS, and the space between it and the footlights has been made to look like a chapel containing a statue hidden by a drape

Strindberg enters with a candle. He hangs a picture of the Virgin centrally on the ladder

Gertrud enters

Strindberg Bring the flowers.

Gertrud exits

Harriet comes in. For the first time we see her with her hair down

Harriet Good morning.
Strindberg Fröken Bosse.

She kneels down to kiss his hand

Harriet I read your play. I didn't sleep all night.
Strindberg (*raising her to her feet*) How can you look like that when you've had no sleep?
Harriet Like what?
Strindberg Beautiful. Radiant.
Harriet I'm under the spell of your play.
Strindberg Tell me what you think.
Harriet What can I say.

dberg Tell me what's good and what's bad.
Harriet I can't.
Strindberg You did read it?
Harriet Oh yes.
Strindberg Give me your impressions before they're washed away by other things.

She can't

Will you play the part? I'm writing it for you.

She moves away to take off her street clothes

Should he end up in a monastery?
Harriet I don't know how to answer.
Strindberg Should he?
Harriet End up in a monastery? It depends.
Strindberg Tell me.
Harriet The woman you made ... created for him ... the Lady ...
Strindberg Say it.
Harriet Could she reconcile him to life?
Strindberg You've understood.
Harriet If she showed him all the brightness and goodness in the world ...
Strindberg Without her he can't see it.
Harriet But it's *there*.
Strindberg Go on.
Harriet If she took him by the hand ...
Strindberg Yes.
Harriet (*not taking his hand*) Would he let himself be led?
Strindberg He wants to be led.
Harriet But would he let her lead him?
Strindberg Oh yes.
Harriet He must stay in the world. He has things to accomplish. Great things.
Strindberg You think so?
Harriet You're asking a lot of her. What if she isn't strong enough?
Strindberg She is.
Harriet What will happen if she disappoints him?
Strindberg She won't.
Harriet But if she does ——
Strindberg His bond with humanity is a rope that's so frayed ...
Harriet She longs to make him feel at peace with other people, but if she fails ——

Strindberg She won't fail.
Harriet If he ignores all her forebodings and takes her calmly by the hand ...
Strindberg (*still not taking her hand*) Yes?
Harriet And walks with her towards the future ...
Strindberg Yes?

*Gertrud enters with flowerpots, which she arranges around the picture.
She exits*

Harriet What are they for?
Strindberg You're not in this scene. I'm alone in my room. It's my cult of
the Madonna. It became a twilight habit.
Harriet What did?
Strindberg Every evening I pulled the blinds down and arranged the plants.
I sat inside the circle and wrote to her.
Harriet Wrote to the Virgin Mary?

*He pulls the drape aside to reveal a life-size costumed dummy wearing a silk
dress with a bustle and the blonde wig from the props table*

Strindberg I couldn't write anything else. Love letters.
Harriet You loved her so much.
Strindberg Adored her.
Harriet I had a dream last night. We were all here, rehearsing. And a woman
was sitting on the stage, there, listening. I knew who she was, knew I had
to go over, speak to her. You didn't see her. I was scared, but I made myself
go to her. She was dead. She was sitting there, dead, and ——
Strindberg And you couldn't move.
Harriet (*surprised*) That's right.
Strindberg (*gently*) Last night, after you left, I possessed you three times.
Harriet Don't say that.
Strindberg I want to be led. Lead me.
Harriet I can't.
Strindberg You can if I teach you.
Harriet We can't talk about this now. (*Staring into the stalls*) Not here. He'll
arrive any minute. He may already be here, listening.
Strindberg (*also staring into the stalls*) He's not called till half-past. I
wanted to see you alone.
Harriet Gertrud?
Strindberg (*laughing gently*) No-one can hear us.
Harriet You frighten me.
Strindberg Only because you don't know me.

Harriet I don't mind if you have fantasies about me. I'm an actress. But that's fantasy. I wasn't with you when I wasn't with you.

Strindberg What I see with my inner eye is more real than what passes for reality. When I see my pillow assuming your shape, your shape is there. If you say that's only fantasy, I say: "What do you mean 'only'?" We can be together at any time.

Harriet No.

Strindberg Yes. You know that. It couldn't have happened without your consent.

Harriet No.

Strindberg I think it was you who taught me.

Harriet No.

Strindberg I never used to be like this. You *know* what you do to me. Sit down.

Harriet (*sitting*) Are you hypnotizing me?

Strindberg You're the enchantress.

Harriet Are you?

Strindberg It's you. You're the one who's doing it. Stand up.

She does

Harriet You're bewitching me.

Strindberg I'm doing nothing. You're doing it.

Harriet August? Gusten?

Strindberg Take me in your arms. You don't need to move or say anything. Just wait. Do nothing. Wait.

She moves towards him. He turns to someone invisible in the space Harriet indicated when she talked about her dream

⸱No. Don't come now. Not now. You always spoil everything. You shouldn't be here.

Harriet Who are you talking to?

Strindberg You have nothing to do with me. Not any more.

Harriet Is she there?

Strindberg (*ignoring Harriet to argue with the invisible Siri*) I am entitled to write about it ... It was my marriage ... It's *not* revenge, it's exorcism. I'm going to stop you from spoiling everything.

Harriet She's not there.

Strindberg You behaved atrociously. But I don't mind. I'm grateful for the appalling things you did. Sincerely. Without them I couldn't have written so well about marriage. But I don't want you here. Go away.

Bengt enters

Ah, Herr Anders. What time did I call you? It doesn't matter. (*Calling*)
Gertrud! (*To Bengt*) I've changed my mind. I was going to do the Madonna
sequence.

Gertrud enters with coffee

Get rid of those flowerpots. Quickly.
Bengt I'll help.
Strindberg The scene about the wretchedness of a woman's life.
Harriet That's what they're all about.
Strindberg The picnic scene.
Harriet Oh, I know. May I look at your script, Gertrud?
Gertrud Yes, Fröken Bosse. Of course.
Strindberg Let's start.
Gertrud Just a moment, Herr Strindberg. I'm not ready.

Harriet, Bengt and Gertrud make hasty preparations for the picnic scene

Harriet Are you ready?
Strindberg Go ahead.
Harriet Isn't it wretched?

Bengt enters in hat and coat, carrying a picnic basket

Bengt What?
Harriet Having no aim in life, nothing to live for.
Bengt (*spreading a rug on the ground*) But my dear Siri! What about your
daughter?
Harriet What?
Bengt Well, she may have brothers and sisters.
Harriet You're like everyone else. They all think I've been put into the world
just to breed babies. What am I supposed to do once they're born? I have
two maids and a nurse. How much work does that leave?
Bengt When your daughter goes to school, she'll need guidance.
Harriet I want to live my own life.
Bengt You want to go on the stage.
Harriet Why shouldn't I go on the stage?
Bengt How can a baroness be an actress?
Harriet That's what's driving me mad. Why are you smiling?

Bengt I'm happy when I'm with you.
Harriet I trust you with my naked soul, and you ——
Bengt I'm not laughing at you.
Harriet Laughter I could understand, but you cover your face with a mask, with sarcasm.
Bengt I'm smiling because I'm happy. I love you.
Harriet You despise me.
Bengt I adore you.
Harriet You thought I kept you waiting on purpose.
Bengt It doesn't matter if you did.
Harriet I didn't. You're always so suspicious.
Bengt Siri, I love you. You love me, and I can't believe my luck. So I invent reasons for being anxious.
Harriet What would I have gained by provoking you? Sometimes I feel like taking your head in my hands and kissing your forehead, with a kiss that would be perfectly pure. I'd love you the same way if you were a woman.
Strindberg Stop. I never wrote that.
Harriet It doesn't work, does it?
Strindberg Why did you say it?
Harriet I was trying something out. She still loves him like a sister, and haven't got it right yet, this non-sexual love. But I agree with you. It sounded wrong.
Strindberg You deliberately said something I didn't write?
Harriet Don't worry. I won't say it in performance.
Strindberg You shouldn't have said it in rehearsal.
Harriet That's how I work. I try to make myself feel free.
Strindberg You're not free. Not to change my words.
Harriet I need to believe they're my words. Isn't that obvious?
Strindberg No.
Harriet To play the part truthfully, I have to speak the words as if they're mine — not yours.
Strindberg It's called acting.
Harriet I can't make your words into mine unless I feel free to make mine into yours. You're not a woman, and you're much older.
Strindberg These things I'm writing about — they happened to me.
Harriet Women aren't things that happen to men.
Strindberg I couldn't have written this play without knowing Siri. Don't assume you know her better than I do.
Harriet If my line had worked, you wouldn't have noticed you didn't write it.
Strindberg Of course I would.
Harriet You didn't notice earlier on when I put a line in.
Strindberg What? What line?

Harriet (*quoting it*) What am I supposed to do once they're born?
Strindberg I wrote that.
Harriet You see? You think it's your line.
Strindberg Gertrud, is that line in the script or not?
Gertrud Well, Herr Strindberg, I didn't say anything because you hate it
when I interrupt a scene, but I made a mark to show that Fröken Bosse had
added some words. (*Turning pages and holding out the prompt script*) I
didn't have time to write them down, but I was going to mention it.
Harriet Shall I leave the line in?
Strindberg No. It's superfluous. (*Going*) Gertrud, you had something to
show me.
Gertrud What was that, Herr Strindberg?
Strindberg Costumes. Designs. A letter. In the office.

He goes without waiting for her

Gertrud I liked it better with your line in.

Gertrud exits

Bengt Are you all right?
Harriet Fine.
Bengt You look different.
Harriet I've got my hair down.
Bengt But you're all right?
Harriet Fine.
Bengt Did you go?
Harriet I didn't stay long. Nothing happened.
Bengt I was worried.
Harriet He's different at home, more relaxed. Here he's always on edge.
And he makes everyone else jumpy too.
Bengt Playwrights should never direct their own work. Cigarette?

*She shakes her head. He puts his cigarettes away without taking one for
himself*

Harriet It was odd this morning before you got here.
Bengt What happened?
Harriet Last night, after I'd gone, he thought I was still there.
Bengt When you weren't?
Harriet This morning he said we could be together without being together.
Bengt You mean like telepathy? I saw that in a circus. It's extraordinary. But
it seems to work.

Harriet He was talking about pillows.
Bengt Pillows? What did he say about pillows?
Harriet Something about seeing me. His pillows take on the shape of my body. It was rather embarrassing.
Bengt What does he do when he thinks the pillows are you?
Harriet I don't know.
Bengt What does he say he does?
Harriet He said he possessed me three times.
Bengt Well, it's not hard to imagine what he does.
Harriet I'm sorry. I shouldn't have told you.
Bengt Fröken Bosse, I'm glad you told me. I want you to know that I'll do anything for you. Anything at all. To help you, protect you. Anything. What would you like me to do?
Harriet Nothing.
Bengt We must have a proper talk. Come to my rooms as soon as the rehearsal's over. All right?
Harriet All right.
Bengt I know what I can do.
Harriet What?
Bengt When he comes, leave me alone with him.
Harriet What will you do?
Bengt Let him know that I know.
Harriet Know what?
Bengt I'll tell him you've confided in me.
Harriet No, don't.
Bengt You don't want me to?
Harriet What good will it do?
Bengt It will stop him. He'll know he hasn't got you at his mercy. That you aren't alone.
Harriet (*after hesitating*) All right. Try not to hurt him. What will you say?
Bengt That you're glad to be in his play, but his relationship with you must be strictly professional. No more than that.
Harriet You won't say anything offensive or hurtful?
Bengt I promise.
Harriet All right. (*She is about to go*)

Gertrud enters

Gertrud Rest of today's rehearsals are cancelled. Tomorrow at ten.
Bengt Gertrud, would you be good enough to ask Herr Strindberg to come on stage?
Gertrud What?

Bengt I'd like a word with him.
Gertrud You want me to tell him that?
Bengt Yes. Please.
Gertrud Well, if you want me to.

Gertrud exits

Harriet exits

Waiting nervously, Bengt lights a cigarette

After a moment Strindberg appears

Strindberg What is this?
Bengt I wanted a quick word.
Strindberg Well?
Bengt It's about Fröken Bosse.
Strindberg My dear friend. I'm so glad. I need your advice.
Bengt She wants you to know ——
Strindberg There are times when men, if they're dealing with a woman, when a man needs another man as a sounding board. May I speak to you as a friend?
Bengt Of course, but what I have to tell you ——
Strindberg I've never been under so much tension. I'm living only for her. Other men just use a woman, but all my thoughts are revolving around Bosse.
Bengt But her feelings for you, Herr Strindberg ——
Strindberg She can restore my faith in human goodness. I feel as if we're engaged. Today I chose furniture for our bedroom out of Bodafors's catalogue. And I've bought new clothes. This shirt is new.
Bengt It's very nice. But what I wanted ——
Strindberg But suppose the whole thing is make-believe? (*Pause*) What then? Last night I possessed her three times, but was it an angel in my bed or a demon? I didn't know till I looked through the window at the crosses formed by lamps on the Slottsbacken. I was safe then, but the smell of incense was so strong I was still afraid. Could a demon send out beneficent irradiations?
Bengt Shouldn't you talk to someone who knows you?
Strindberg Who?
Bengt I don't know. You must have many friends.
Strindberg Can you name one? I've never lacked enemies. Stockholm is full of them, but who are my friends? Please give me your advice. I think she's

been abusing my gift of all that's finest in me. She's been talking about me
to another man, and when he defiles her with his glances, he disgraces me.
Are you capable of doing something you consider evil?
Bengt No. If I think it's evil. No.
Strindberg If a woman belongs to another man, you'd never try to tempt her
away?
Bengt A woman doesn't belong to a man until they're married.
Strindberg Ha! So until the vows are spoken, any man has the right to tempt
her away? You believe that?
Bengt Herr Strindberg.
Strindberg What?
Bengt I don't know what to say.
Strindberg Should I trust her if another man loves her ——?
Bengt But Fröken Bosse ——
Strindberg — would never talk about me to another man?
Bengt How would I know?

A pair of hands starts clapping in the auditorium. It is Harriet

Strindberg (*peering into the darkness as the applause continues*) This is a
private theatre. A play is in rehearsal. You have no right to be here.
Harriet (*from the stalls*) You were both superb. (*Coming forward to the
stage*) Why do they say heroic acting is in decline? What panache! What
bravado! What loyalty!
Bengt How long have you been there?
Harriet Thank you for speaking up so bravely on my behalf.
Bengt I'm sorry. I ——
Harriet You should both be ashamed.
Bengt I'm sorry.
Strindberg Fröken Bosse ——
Harriet How dare you discuss me in a theatre?
Strindberg This is a private rehearsal.
Harriet If I can sit in the stalls unnoticed, so can anyone. Now I know what
Siri will feel if she comes to the play.
Strindberg (*to Bengt*) You'd better leave us.
Bengt (*to Harriet*) Do you want me to go?
Harriet I don't care what you do.
Bengt If you don't care, I'll go. If you want to know, I find all this acutely
embarrassing. (*About to leave*) Just one thing, Herr Strindberg. I read *The
Madman's Defence* before I met you. I think you should tell Fröken Bosse
about the rape, and how you got Siri pregnant.

Bengt exits

Harriet Rape?
Strindberg You see? I told him to give free rein to the malice inside him. What an obedient young man!
Harriet Rape?
Strindberg I'll tell you both stories. Anyone can read them. They're in print. Which one would you like first? Rape or impregnation?
Harriet I don't want to hear either. (*She is about to leave*)
Strindberg Do you want to give up the part?

She hesitates

The first time Siri visited me in my room she told me Jarl had left her alone ever since the baby. One child was enough. I was aroused by these intimate confessions. When I made advances, she offered no resistance till the crucial moment. Then she freed herself and left. But she came back. Again and again the torture was repeated—kisses, cuddles, passion, nothing. She was treating me like a eunuch, and when I took her by force, all she said was: "That's the end of the proud Baroness". That was the rape. When she moved out of Jarl's house, I tried to protect her reputation. I said she wanted a divorce so she could go on the stage. There was too much of a scandal for her to work here, so I got her a part at the Holberg in Copenhagen. She rewarded me with news about her friendship with a young musician. She even sent me love letters he wrote. When she came back, she was wearing black silk stockings on legs that were fuller than before. White knees shone through the blackness and dainty ankles. I was overwhelmed, but she was worried about pregnancy. I was working in the Royal Library, and I said I'd found a book on how to cheat nature. I also told her I had an organic defect that made the risk even smaller. She said I could do whatever I wished if I took full responsibility.
Harriet At last! Now I know how to play her. You should have told me all that before.
Strindberg What do you mean?
Harriet I didn't know what you were like when you were in love. All I have to do is react.

They are staring at each other

Strindberg All you ever have to do is react. That's what I do when I'm with you. Last night, you didn't find it embarrassing when I wept? I thought you would. I know what people say about me. They think I'm a woman-hater and a monster. You don't expect to see a monster weep. Were you disappointed?

Harriet I was moved. Why did you weep?

Strindberg Because I could. It's such a long time since I wept! When you're utterly miserable, you can't. A glimmer of hope is necessary. That's what you've done for me. I was in deep darkness, but the light came when you kissed my hand. Do you like children?

Harriet Of course.

Strindberg (*kneeling in front of her*) Will you have a baby for me?

Harriet gets up and scours the auditorium. Strindberg stays on his knees

(*Quietly*) Have we been observed?

Harriet (*answering the first of his two questions*) Yes.

Strindberg I'm sorry. It was my fault. Who's there?

Harriet (*kneeling opposite him*) My answer is yes I will.

Strindberg You will?

Harriet Yes. Thank you.

Strindberg How strange life is! I'd completely given up hope.

The Lights fade to Black-out

ACT II

SCENE 1

The same

New furniture has been brought on to the stage —the furniture that the actors will use in the production. This includes a bench, chairs, a table, a desk, statues and two lamps

Gertrud is arranging a bench for the garden set. Bengt enters in outdoor clothes

Gertrud Good morning, Herr Anders. How are you today?

Bengt (*cheerfully*) Extremely well, thank you, Gertrud. And I hope you are. You needn't bother to do that. You'll find it's not necessary. Are the Strindbergs here? I have news for them.

Gertrud No, it's only ten to ten. Why didn't you go to the wedding?

Bengt Did you?

Gertrud Of course. And he gave me money to buy spring flowers. I stood in the Djürgarden and scattered them on him and Fröken Bosse when the carriage passed. Him and Fru Strindberg I should say. Don't tell her he gave me money. He wants her to think it was my idea.

Bengt I won't tell her. Did she look good?

Gertrud Like a fairy princess. Long white veil. I must get on.

Bengt I told you — don't bother. We aren't going to rehearse.

Gertrud Oh, yes. The rehearsal's at ten.

Bengt It's going to be cancelled.

Gertrud What do you mean? Shush!

Pause

Strindberg and Harriet enter in outdoor clothes

Bengt Congratulations!

Harriet Good morning.

Strindberg We missed you at the reception.

Bengt I couldn't make it. Let me give the bride a belated kiss. (*He intends to kiss her cheek but kisses her gloved hand*)

Harriet Thank you.
Strindberg (*to Gertrud*) Why isn't the set ready? I want to work on the
garden scene.
Bengt Entirely my fault, Herr Strindberg. I stopped Gertrud.

Strindberg turns, about to become angry

I've been offered a job in Malmö. I'm sorry.
Strindberg What job?
Bengt Herr Larssen wants me for *The Wild Duck.*
Strindberg Huh!
Bengt And he's got a theatre. He wants me to play Gregers Werle.
Strindberg That swinish play!
Bengt Herr Strindberg ——
Strindberg Symbolic pigswill!
Bengt I'd rather be in a play by you than a Norwegian play, but I want to be
in a play audiences see.
Strindberg My play will be seen. We have a theatre.
Bengt Since when?
Strindberg Everything will be settled today.
Bengt Which theatre?
Strindberg The Lundberg.
Bengt Opening when?
Strindberg In three weeks. I'm meeting Gustafsen at lunchtime.
Bengt Give me a moment to think.
Strindberg What about? You have a choice between my staging of my new
play or a third-rate staging of a third-rate play by that pig of a Norwegian.
Harriet Give him some time.
Bengt Thank you, Fru Strindberg. I'll go to my dressing-room.

He exits

Harriet It'll be all right. Just don't push too hard.
Strindberg He's jealous.
Harriet He needs security.
Strindberg We'll give him security.
Harriet We can now. But we haven't yet.
Strindberg I'll speak to him. (*He starts to leave*)
Harriet Let me.
Strindberg Can you persuade him?
Harriet Some things I can do better than you.
Strindberg Many things. (*He embraces her*)

Harriet Give me as long as it takes. (*She is about to go*)

Bengt comes back

Bengt I'm sorry, but I'm going to play Gergers Werle.
Strindberg Gertrud, come and show me the costume designs. (*To Bengt*)
Give yourself more time.
Gertrud What costume designs, Herr Strindberg?
Strindberg The ones for Act Two. Come.

He exits

Gertrud They're the same as Act One.

She follows him

Harriet I'm sorry.
Bengt What for, Fru Strindberg?
Harriet Don't call me that.
Bengt I can no longer call you Fröken Bosse.
Harriet In the theatre I shall always be Fröken Bosse. To you I shall always
be Harriet.
Bengt Never once have I called you Harriet.
Harriet You could have. We've had intimate conversations.
Bengt You look different.
Harriet I'm not different.
Bengt You're a married woman.
Harriet I feel the same.
Bengt Are you all right?
Harriet Yes.
Bengt You don't sound all right.
Harriet How can I answer that?
Bengt Tell me what you feel.
Harriet I know what you'd like me to say.
Bengt What?
Harriet That I've made a mistake. That I knew all along it was wrong. That
I know what your feelings are. That I feel the same ... Be kind to me.
Bengt How can I? What you want from me has nothing to do with what I want
from you.
Harriet Are you sure?
Bengt You think I don't know why he left us together?
Harriet So that I can persuade you to stay.

Bengt Obviously. I know there are lots of other young actors who'd jump
at the chance of playing Strindberg opposite Fru Strindberg in a play by
Strindberg directed by Strindberg. But what a nuisance to start all over
again when I'm half broken in.

Harriet Broken in?

Bengt Yes. Like you. Broken in. You've married a man who hates women.

Harriet He loves me. You're the one who hates me.

Bengt I hate you?

Harriet No, but you hate him.

Bengt Yes.

Harriet Why?

Bengt He's your husband.

Harriet I don't belong to him.

Bengt But ...

Harriet Say it ... Are you jealous?

Bengt He's got you and I ...

Harriet What?

Bengt You know what.

Harriet You want me?

Bengt This is torture. You know I do. Yes. I want you.

Harriet You say that. Can I believe you?

He hesitates. They seem to be on the point of embracing

Bengt This is mad. What are we doing?

Harriet What we want to do. We were mad before.

Bengt You're married to him.

Harriet What does that mean?

Bengt It means you're his wife.

Harriet What does *that* mean?

Bengt It doesn't mean I don't want you.

Harriet It doesn't mean I don't want you.

They hold on to each other

Bengt I never want to be further away from you than this.

Harriet You're so young.

Bengt I'm older than you are.

Harriet Only in age.

Bengt He could come on stage any second. What shall we do?

Harriet We'll take one step at a time.

Bengt I love you.

Harriet I don't think I'll ever love a man.
Bengt You're going to love me.
Harriet Don't say anything to him.
Bengt I won't.
Harriet (*moving away*) We must carry on as if nothing's happened.
Bengt That won't be easy.
Harriet Whatever you feel, use it. (*Calling*) Gertrud?
Bengt What do you mean?
Harriet In the play. Use it.

Gertrud enters

Herr Strindberg wants you to set up the museum scene.
Gertrud He didn't say that.
Harriet Tell him Herr Anders is staying. No, I'll tell him. Set up the museum scene.

She exits

Bengt sits on the bench

Gertrud The museum scene!
Bengt I'll help you.
Gertrud Thanks. Let's position this first. Are you going to help?

He gets up and they move a packing case, constructing a makeshift statue on it with chairs

Harriet comes back with Strindberg

Strindberg Not the museum scene, Gertrud, the garden scene.
Harriet We want the museum scene. Bengt and I.
Strindberg (*to Gertrud*) Set up the museum scene.
Gertrud It's ready.

Harriet and Bengt sit down on the bench

Ready? All right? Curtain going up, curtain up!

Bengt kisses Harriet's eyes, her cheeks, her lips. She doesn't resist but she doesn't respond, except by smiling

Bengt The time has come to tell him. I can't share you with another man.
Harriet Keep your voice down. We're in a public place.
Bengt There's nobody here. I adore you. I love your golden hair, your
    wonderful eyes, your silky skin, your shoulders, the tiniest feet in Sweden.
Harriet Should we cut that line? My feet are quite big.
Strindberg Don't stop.
Bengt Tiniest feet in Sweden. I want to kiss your throat. I want to smother
    you with kisses. My love for you gives me the strength of a god.
Harriet Relax. You've been ill.
Bengt Beware the sick lion. I want you, and I'm going to have you. I can't
    go on pretending to be your husband's friend. He detests me — the son of
    a servant. And I detest him — the over-privileged baron. Why should he
    have two women while we have to meet in museums?
Harriet I wanted to tell him. You said no.
Bengt The time wasn't ripe. Now it is.
Strindberg Stop. (*To Harriet*) What this scene needs is more contrast
    between his mood and yours.
Harriet You don't think it's a bit overwritten?
Strindberg What?
Harriet It's the most rhetorical sequence in the play.
Strindberg Of course it is. I'm young, and I'm in love. That's how a young
    lover speaks.
Harriet No-one's spoken to me like that.
Strindberg This is thirty years ago.
Harriet It can't be.
Strindberg Twenty-four years ago.
Bengt I think Fröken Bosse is right.
Strindberg What?
Harriet I know what felt wrong. (*To Bengt*) I want to kiss your throat.
Bengt I want to kiss your throat. (*Kissing her eyes, her cheeks, her lips*)

Harriet kisses him on the mouth

Strindberg No, don't kiss him.
Harriet Very well, but ask yourself what's attracting me to you. A whole
    dimension of you is missing. Just now, when you said: "Don't kiss him",
    you showed how vulnerable you are. Why hide that from the audience? A
    man's only irresistible if he's vulnerable.
Bengt That's true.
Harriet Why not put more of your soft side into the play?
Strindberg Don't give me lessons in playwriting.
Harriet That's the tone exactly. Hurt and defensive. Write something like
    that for Bengt.

Bengt Only don't forget we're opening in three weeks.
Strindberg (*after a moment's thought*) Gertrud, the dog scene.
Harriet Why should we do the dog scene now?

Gertrud waits

Strindberg The dog scene.

Gertrud starts moving statues, rearranging chairs and positioning the table while Harriet looks at a script

    Ready?
Gertrud (*arranging crockery and cutlery*) Right.

Harriet and Bengt sit down at the table as before, and mime eating soup. Gertrud yelps

Harriet Poor Waffles!
Bengt This is torture.
Harriet He'd be quiet if only he could come in.
Bengt He's not coming in here while I'm eating.
Harriet I'm sure he'd be good.
Bengt The subject is closed.
Harriet All right.

More yelping from Gertrud

Bengt Be quiet!

Louder yelping

    Are we going to have this every mealtime?
Harriet What can I do?
Bengt Rat poison?
Harriet Sorry, could we stop? Last time we did this, you told me Waffles used to belong to Merta ——
Strindberg Marta.
Harriet My daughter Marta, who died when she was three. I should have thought about that, but I haven't, what with the wedding and everything. I'm sorry. Could we leave this scene until I've had time to think about Marta?
Strindberg You should have taken time.

Harriet Have you written the line?

Strindberg What line?

Harriet The line about Marta. I told you, Marta makes a difference. I need a line about her.

Strindberg I'll think about it.

He exits

(Off; calling) Gertrud, we'll break.

Gertrud exits

Bengt Harriet? *(He wants to embrace her)*

Harriet I can't.

Bengt When you said we must carry on as if nothing's happened ... for how long?

Silence

You know your marriage isn't going to last.

Harriet Don't say that.

Bengt You're unhappy.

Harriet No. He was a wonderful fiancé, like a cavalier. He sent flowers and presents. Thought of everything to please me. He even took me out to dinner. You know how he hates eating in public.

Bengt He may have been a good fiancé. He's incapable of being a good husband.

Harriet I promised to make him happy.

Bengt He's a woman-hater.

Harriet He's not a woman-hater, except on paper. And in the mind.

Bengt Isn't the mind rather important?

Harriet It's not too late to change him. With Gusten nothing is static.

Bengt In that case you have no problems.

Harriet It'll be all right. You'll see.

Bengt I wish you luck. In fact I'll help. I'll tell you how to make it work. He needs a woman he can worship, but you must also be submissive. Not too submissive, or he'll get bored. Be strong when he feels weak, and weak when he feels strong. Be seductive sometimes, and sometimes seem virginal. Be patient and tolerant, but never let him suspect you're being patient and tolerant, or that you've seen through him. Have strong feelings, but never disagree with him. Be friendly to the people he likes, and turn against them when he does. That's all for now. I'll give you more help later.

Harriet Don't bother.
Bengt You know Siri's back in Sweden?
Harriet What? Siri?
Bengt She's in Malmö, at the Lorensberg. I didn't meet her, but she's going
to play Mrs Soerby in *The Wild Duck*.

Fade to Black-out

SCENE 2

Strindberg enters in his overcoat, distraught

Strindberg Gertrud! Gertrud!

He exits

Gertrud enters. She takes her coat off and starts to sweep the stage

(*Off*) Gertrud!
Gertrud I'm here.
Strindberg (*off*) Where?
Gertrud On stage.

Strindberg enters

Strindberg Have you seen Fru Strindberg this morning?
Gertrud I've only just got in. (*She looks at her watch*)
Strindberg Where's Herr Anders?
Gertrud He's not called till ten fifteen.
Strindberg What time is it?
Gertrud Ten to. Which scene shall I set up?
Strindberg I don't know. (*He moves about restlessly*)
Gertrud Would you like a nice hot cup of coffee?
Strindberg No.
Gertrud Tea?
Strindberg No. All right, yes.

Gertrud is about to go

No, coffee. Very strong. Why aren't they here?
Gertrud (*on the point of going*) Isn't Fru Strindberg with you?
Strindberg What do you mean? Of course she's with me. What are you
talking about? Go on. Go and make the coffee.

Gertrud Sorry.

Gertrud exits

Strindberg Gertrud.

She comes back

I'm sorry I spoke to you like that. Take your glasses off.

She does so

You have such beautiful eyes.
Gertrud Are you all right, Herr Strindberg?
Strindberg Of course I'm all right. How are you?
Gertrud Me?
Strindberg No, Gertrud, I'm not all right.
Gertrud Is there anything I can do?
Strindberg You'd better make some coffee.

She puts her glasses on and goes

Strindberg paces about. He keeps taking out his pocket watch

Eventually Bengt arrives

Bengt Good morning, Herr Strindberg.
Strindberg What have you to tell me?
Bengt Well, I think I'm rounding the corner. At first I was too intimidated.
  You don't realize how daunting it is to be cast as a younger version of the
  author when the author's also directing. At first, as you know, I thought the
  various aspects of my character didn't fit together ——
Strindberg Where's my wife?
Bengt Isn't she with you?
Strindberg Would I ask if she were?
Bengt She's not with me.
Strindberg I can see that. Where is she?
Bengt I don't know.
Strindberg When did you last see her?
Bengt On Saturday. Here. At rehearsal.
Strindberg I want the truth.
Bengt That is the truth. Don't you believe me?

Strindberg Tell her you know about her assaults on me. She's got to leave me alone.

Bengt She's not with me.

Strindberg The attacks on my stomach were so violent last night I had to lie down. I slept for a bit, and when I woke up I tried to pray, but that didn't stop her. Tell her. If she's with you, she doesn't need me ——

Bengt She's not.

Strindberg — and if she comes when I'm asleep, I can't control myself. Why should I? She's my wife, and in this hell she shares with you ——

Bengt She's not with me.

Strindberg Then where is she?

Bengt I can't tell you.

Strindberg I'm her husband. I have rights.

Bengt I can't tell you because I don't know.

Strindberg How can I get her back when I don't know where she is.

Bengt When did you last see her?

Strindberg Last night. She still wants me. I tried to resist, but at midnight she was there again, and she tasted like roses. No, it must have been later. I heard guns firing a salute. Did she come back to you?

Bengt She's not with me.

Strindberg Then where is she?

Bengt When did you last see her? Really see her?

Strindberg Saturday. She was in a strange mood. She's easily upset when a man speaks in a certain way. At nine a note arrived, saying she'd gone. Life is a cruel joke. In the morning I went for a walk. On the way back I found a hairpin and an undamaged horseshoe. At home I read what I'd written in my diary, and I blessed her for bringing me joy. But if my woman traps me into picturing the sexual acts of other men, she's making me into a pervert. How can I keep my soul out of the filth?

Bengt I don't know what to say.

Harriet enters in a cloak, carrying a travelling bag

Neither of them sees her

Strindberg Love involves the basest organs, but if I arouse the beauty of a young female soul, how can she welcome into the centre of her being an organ designed for the drainage of another male body? How can she?

Bengt I don't know what to say.

Strindberg Tell me what you feel. Am I right?

Bengt sees Harriet. Then Strindberg does

Harriet Good morning. I'm sorry I'm late.
Strindberg Late?
Harriet Isn't there a rehearsal?

Gertrud enters with coffee

Gertrud Good morning, Fru Strindberg.
Harriet Good morning, Gertrud.
Gertrud (*giving the coffee to Bengt*) Would you like a cup too, Fru
Strindberg?
Harriet Thanks, Gertrud, I'd love a cup.
Bengt (*giving her his*) Have this.
Harriet Thank you.
Gertrud I'll get another cup, Herr Anders. I won't be a minute. There's some
in the pot.

She exits

Strindberg Where were you?
Harriet Nowhere. I'm here.
Strindberg Herr Anders, be good enough to leave us.
Harriet No. Don't go.
Strindberg I wish to speak to my wife.
Harriet I came here to rehearse. Let's rehearse.
Strindberg We can rehearse later. We have to talk.
Harriet I don't want to talk. I want to rehearse.
Strindberg As you wish. (*Shouting*) Gertrud! Where are you?
Bengt She's getting more coffee.
Gertrud (*off*) Just coming.

She enters with coffee

If it's not hot enough, Herr Anders, just tell me, and I'll warm it up.
Strindberg Gertrud, we're trying to do the scene with the funeral sweets.

Bengt sits at the table. Harriet paces about

Harriet I'm so hungry.
Bengt I'm sorry there's no food.
Harriet We should have stayed at my mother's.
Bengt The perfect love-nest! She peeps through the keyhole.

Harriet She does no such thing.
Bengt I wouldn't put it past her.
Harriet Don't talk like that. Jarl never got on with her, but he never said things like that.
Bengt You keep talking about him.
Harriet Because you keep forgetting I was a baroness with servants, and I never went hungry.

She is interrupted by a sound which turns out to be coming from Gertrud — she is sobbing

Bengt Are you all right?
Gertrud (*unable to stop*) Yes.
Strindberg Gertrud, what's the matter?
Gertrud Nothing. Don't take any notice.
Strindberg But how can we rehearse if ——?
Harriet Just go. Leave me alone with her. (*She puts her arms round Gertrud*)
Strindberg Well, if you think ——
Harriet Both of you. Go. Go on.
Strindberg We'll be in Bengt's dressing-room. Come with me.

Strindberg and Bengt exit

Harriet It's all right. They've gone.
Gertrud (*still weeping*) I'm sorry.
Harriet It's all right.
Gertrud I'm so sorry. It's the first time I've ever ...
Harriet It's all right. I know.
Gertrud You don't know.
Harriet Did something happen?
Gertrud Nothing really.
Harriet Look, have my handkerchief. It's nice and big. Now, what happened?
Gertrud Nothing. It was the second time.
Harriet What was?
Gertrud Herr Strindberg. He said "Take your glasses off". (*She blows her nose*) It's the second time he made me do it. You don't know what it's like to be me.
Harriet I know.
Gertrud You don't know. You've always had men running after you.
Harriet That's not always as nice as you think.
Gertrud It's nicer than ... (*more sobbing*)

Harriet Don't, Gertrud. I'm so fond of you. I hate to see you like this. You're so good at making other people feel better. You deserve to have someone who can comfort you.

Gertrud I'm sorry.

Harriet It's all right.

Gertrud Look, I've stopped crying. Shall I take this home and wash it for you?

Harriet Keep it. It's a present. Shall I call the men?

Gertrud No, not yet. Please. Yes. I'm all right now.

Harriet Are you sure?

Gertrud Yes. Wait a minute. All right.

Harriet exits

Gertrud blows her nose again, takes a mirror from her handbag and dabs powder on her cheeks, which are still wet

Harriet comes back with Strindberg and Bengt

Strindberg You all right, Gertrud?

Gertrud (*barely able to get the words out*) Yes, I'm sorry.

Strindberg It's all right. Don't worry. Now, where shall we go from?

Gertrud Do you want to take ... (*she sobs*)

Harriet Gertrud. (*She puts her arm round Gertrud*)

Gertrud I'll be all right. Do you want to take it from "I never went hungry"?

Strindberg Fine.

Harriet and Bengt take up their positions

Harriet I was a baroness with servants, and I never went hungry. Whatever you say about my mother, at least she taught me how to behave. (*At the window*) I wish it would get dark.

Bengt Are you in such a hurry to be back with her?

Harriet Impatience is a luxury I can no longer afford. I'm in prison there, and it's the same here.

Bengt It'll be better once the divorce comes through.

Harriet I've eaten nothing since lunchtime.

Bengt Why not go home to your mother's and have some supper?

Harriet Alone? Unescorted?

Bengt starts piling papers, notebooks, bundles of letters tied in ribbon, faded flowers, etc., on top of the desk and rummaging through the drawers

Bengt We shouldn't be seen together..
Harriet Thank you very much. I suppose you'll be glad when I've gone.
Then you can get on with your writing ... I put that line in. Is that all right?
Strindberg Are you going to take it out later?
Harriet If it doesn't help the scene, I will. Otherwise, I'll leave it in. All right?
Strindberg All right.

Gertrud writes in the script

Bengt I've often gone to bed hungry. I'm sure you've never done that.
Harriet Should I be grateful for the opportunity?
Bengt There must be something you could eat somewhere.
Harriet You aren't going to find food in there.

Finally he brings out two sweets wrapped in black paper and tinfoil

What on earth?
Bengt They're sweets. Eat them. I kept them in remembrance of a funeral.
Harriet Whose funeral?
Bengt He was Chief Librarian at the Royal Library.

She gingerly unwraps one of the sweets and puts it into her mouth. Then she spits it out

Harriet How long have you had those?
Bengt Less than a year.
Harriet Eugh!
Bengt I thought you could keep sweets any amount of time. Isn't sugar a
preservative?

There is no answer

Siri?
Harriet What?
Bengt Don't be like this. It's no-one's fault. It's society. We've done nothing
wrong. They tolerate adultery and condemn divorce. We're ostracized, but
he's a baron, so anything he does is all right.

Bengt takes her in his arms. She submits at first

I'm glad we didn't stay in your mother's flat. We may both be hungry, but
at least we can do what we feel like.

He wants to make love but she doesn't

Harriet I feel like eating.
Bengt Do you know what I think?
Harriet What?
Bengt He was leading us both by the nose.
Harriet What do you mean?
Bengt He wanted us to fall in love. That's why he made friends with me.
What he wants is a divorce that makes him look like the innocent party.
Then he'll marry Tilda.
Harriet I won't hear a word against him. It was all my fault ... That doesn't
ring true. Why am I defending him?
Strindberg Because that's what she was like. Totally unreasonable.
Harriet It may seem unreasonable to you, but it didn't to her.
Strindberg That's right. She didn't even know when she was being
impossible.
Harriet It's all written from your point of view.
Strindberg Of course it is. I wrote it.
Harriet I knew I shouldn't accept this part.
Strindberg You're the only actress who could play it.
Harriet (*pacing and pondering*) The other problem is the climax of this
scene. We're building towards the revelation that she went on sleeping
with Jarl after she moved out. Did she?
Strindberg Yes.
Harriet How do you know?
Strindberg To her it would have seemed perfectly natural.
Harriet But what happened?
Strindberg I don't know. Probably they had dinner there one night. She
always felt sleepy after a meal. If he'd said: "Why not lie down?" she'd
have gone to the bedroom, and if he wanted to lie down with her, it would
have harmed no-one, so long as I didn't find out.
Harriet How did you find out? You see? You didn't. It may never have
happened.
Strindberg This is a play. Not a biography. I must be true to the characters,
not the facts.
Harriet You're not being fair to *her*.
Strindberg You keep saying that. I know her. You don't.
Harriet I do. I went to see her. That's where I was. Malmö.

Strindberg moves away. Silence

Bengt I do think you might have told us.
Harriet What?
Bengt You should have told us.
Harriet Us?
Bengt Herr Strindberg didn't know where you were.
Strindberg How is she?
Harriet Very thin, and she's got a bad cough. She's had it for months.
Strindberg How much is she drinking?
Harriet She looks too poor to buy drink.
Strindberg She looks poor because she spends all her money on drink.
Harriet You don't know that. You make things up.
Strindberg You shouldn't have gone.
Harriet If you were writing about Finland, you'd go there.
Strindberg Do you need to meet Ophelia and visit Denmark? I can tell you
everything you need to know about Siri.
Harriet You could, but you only tell me what you want me to know. Now
I feel better equipped to play her.
Bengt I can understand that.
Harriet I wasn't expecting her to look so old.
Strindberg She's four years younger than I am.
Harriet She's old for her age. You're young for yours.
Strindberg You should have told me you were going.
Harriet You'd have tried to stop me.
Strindberg You gave me the worst weekend I've ever had. I thought you
were leaving me.
Harriet How can I leave you? I don't know for sure but I think I might
be ... (*she breaks off*)

*His face lights up with happiness and pride as he goes down on his knees,
pressing the side of his head to her stomach. She resists at first but then
submits*

Bengt (*embarrassed*) Are we taking a break? Or is that the end of rehearsals
for today?
Harriet I'm sorry. I forgot you were there.
Bengt It stands me in good stead as an actor. This ability to make myself
transparent. I specialize in playing invisible men.
Harriet And you, Gertrud. I'm sorry. I should have ——
Strindberg My dear friends, please forgive us. It's because we feel so close
to both of you. You're like members of the family. But you're right, Herr
Anders, we must rehearse. I'll tell you what. Choose what you'd most like
to work on. We'll do any scene you pick.

Bengt You want me to choose? All right, the cuckold scene.
Harriet I knew it. As soon as you said: "Choose", I knew which scene he'd want.
Strindberg If you'd rather do something else, I'm sure Herr Anders ——
Harriet No, it's the perfect choice. When I've just told you my news, what could be more appropriate than the cuckold scene? Let's go straight into it.
Strindberg All right, Gertrud, what do we need?

Harriet exits

Gertrud Herr Anders is writing at the desk, and the two lamps are lit.

Bengt sits at the table, as at the beginning of the play, and starts to write

Harriet enters, wearing the blonde wig we saw on the dummy. She has a letter and a torn envelope in her hand. The daylight is fading. They are both more fluent and relaxed than last time

Harriet "A cuckold in the theatre is a comic figure. I too would willingly laugh if someone else were the cuckold."
Bengt I knew you were stealing my letters.
Harriet Why don't you post them yourself?
Bengt I do — the ones I want to arrive. The ones I give you are the ones I want you to read.
Harriet Really? Including this one? Do you really think I'm a lesbian? And a whore?
Bengt You want to have me locked up. That's what you want. In a madhouse.
Harriet I think you'd stopped loving me before we got married.
Bengt I still love you. But this is war, and we must fight to the end.
Gertrud (*prompting*) To the death.
Bengt I always get that wrong ... We must fight to the death, the death, the death. We must fight to the death.
Harriet Do you really believe you aren't Karin's father?
Bengt Siri! Don't do this. You're playing with fire. Are you trying to drive me crazy?
Harriet You're crazy already if you think Karin isn't yours. Who do you think her father is?
Bengt Siri, I warn you. I can destroy you if I have to.
Harriet Listen to yourself. Listen to your voice — what you do to it. You deliberately unbalance yourself. When you were an actor, you failed. You make marriage into a performance, testing, always testing how far you can go.

Bengt At least I know when to stop.
Harriet Not always.
Bengt Do I scare you?
Harriet Not as much as you scare yourself.
Bengt You want me to go on deteriorating? If I die, you get the life insurance, but if I kill myself you don't.
Harriet You won't kill yourself. You're not the type. What do you want?
Bengt I need to be sure of my sanity, but you're the only one who knows whether I'm her father.
Strindberg I think we should take a break and then work on something else. We aren't going to get anywhere with this scene. None of us is in the right mood.
Harriet I'd rather go on. How about you, Bengt?
Bengt We must. We never finish a scene. All right with you, Gertrud?
Gertrud Fine.
Harriet Let's go on.
Bengt I need to be sure of my sanity, but you're the only one who knows whether I'm her father.
Harriet It's not my fault if you still have doubts. The madness is in your brain, not mine.
Bengt If I'm not her father, tell me. I'll forgive you, I swear it. Anything's better than uncertainty.
Harriet If I say she's yours, you don't believe me. If I say she's not, you can get rid of me and keep her.
Bengt If she's not mine, I don't want her.
Harriet Then why say you'll forgive me if I've deceived you?
Bengt Have you?
Harriet You're mad already. You don't believe what you're saying. You're talking yourself into it.
Bengt Siri! Tell me the truth.
Harriet You're crying.
Bengt Women always know who fathered their children.
Harriet There's no need to cry. I told you the truth.
Bengt A man never knows. Men look ridiculous in the street holding a child by the hand and showing off. "This is my child." All they ever know for sure ——
Strindberg That's enough. There's something in the script that's troubling me. We can't go on till I've changed the line.
Harriet Don't stop us now. This scene is working for the first time. Can't you see that?
Strindberg We'll work on it again tomorrow.
Bengt Please can we finish the scene?

Strindberg No. I have to work on the script. Take a break. Fifteen minutes.

Harriet sits by herself, slumped in a corner

Make some tea, Gertrud.
Gertrud Herr Strindberg, in case I forget to remind you and the cast later, tomorrow's call is at the Lundberg. I think you all know that? Ten o'clock at the Lundberg. And we have to stop working there by five-thirty. They need the stage for the evening performance.
Strindberg Right. Thank you, Gertrud. Now make the tea.

Gertrud exits

(*To Bengt*) I hope you're pleased with yourself?
Bengt Yes, I think I'm getting there. What was holding me back was knowing how dissimilar I am to you. Somehow that's ceasing to be a problem. At least, that's what I felt just now.
Strindberg Get off the stage.
Bengt What?
Strindberg You heard.
Bengt Well, in answer to your question, yes, I do feel pleased with myself. When I met you, I was afraid of you. I never thought I could win an argument with you, or get you to the point where you could think of nothing better to say than, "Get off the stage". I obey your order, Herr Direktor, with pleasure.

He exits

Harriet Why did you do that?
Strindberg I must talk to you.
Harriet Can't it wait?
Strindberg No.
Harriet I can't talk here. It's too cold.
Strindberg It's not too cold to rehearse.
Harriet It's much too cold to rehearse.
Strindberg We've been rehearsing here for three weeks.
Harriet I've been cold for three weeks, and I'm too cold to talk. You talk if you want to.
Strindberg Well, stop moving about.
Harriet I'm too cold to stand still.
Strindberg Do you know why I stopped the rehearsal?
Harriet No.

Strindberg Aren't you interested?
Harriet No. I'm cold and hungry and thirsty. I could have gone on working, but I hate quarrels as much as you love them.
Strindberg I stopped because I've written something that isn't true. I need to ask you. Does a woman always know who fathered her child? She doesn't, does she?
Harriet Doesn't she?
Strindberg How can she? If she's sleeping with more than one man before she conceives, how can she? She doesn't know.
Harriet Obviously.
Strindberg Well?
Harriet Well what?
Strindberg Reassure me.
Harriet I've just played that scene.
Strindberg Answer my question.
Harriet What question?
Strindberg Have you been unfaithful?
Harriet Let's go home. I hate this place.
Strindberg We'll never be here again. From tomorrow, the Lundberg.
Harriet Does the Lundberg smell like this?
Strindberg What are you talking about? I can't smell anything.
Harriet All theatres stink.
Strindberg How can an actress hate the smell of theatres?
Harriet Do gravediggers like the smell of corpses? Every night in every theatre different bottoms flop into the same seats, and the same actors go through the same routine of gesturing and posturing and emoting.
Strindberg But ——
Harriet I know! (*Mimicking him*) "It's more real than reality". Gesturing, posturing and emoting. That's what's rotting, and that's what the stink is, and you never get rid of it. Not even by burning the place down. You're not jealous. Not really. You just want a scene because the smell's inside you. You're an addict. Go ahead. Act jealous. I don't care. Take the stage. Play the scene. Strut about. It won't change anything. It's theatre. Whatever you say, whatever I say, you'll go on making scenes. Go on. Emote.
Strindberg Have I made you like this?
Harriet Don't you learn from your plays? This is what poisons your marriages. It's nothing to do with Siri or me. It's you. You hate women. All you want from us is the luxury of feeling betrayed.
Strindberg Luxury!
Harriet You whip yourself into outrage. Then you've got material for a scene. You're like a machine.
Strindberg Machines don't get hurt.
Harriet You manufacture pain and pump it in your plays. They're parasites

that feed on your marriages. I understand Siri because you put me under the same strain. You make women into drama.

Strindberg Yes, I'm a writer. If you're my wife you're a part of me.

Harriet Like the food you eat?

Strindberg Has it come to this?

Harriet I was sorry for you. I really did want to take you by the hand. I thought you were willing to be led. You said I made you feel at peace with other people. Remember? You promised to let me show you brightness and goodness.

Strindberg Where are they? Show me.

Harriet Here.

She presses his hands to her solar plexus. A silence. He wants to accept this

Strindberg You're too young. You don't know what lies ahead. You're living in the first act, and you think it's a comedy. It's not even a tragedy. It's a farce, aimed at fooling us into populating the planet. A farce! People aren't born evil — life debases them. There's nothing that isn't worthless. Nothing! Life is illusion, and we'll find truth in another existence. Let's go home. We can't work any more today. We'll make a fresh start in the morning at the Lundberg. A new theatre, a new start, a new life beginning. We'll have the baby. We'll go home now and eat and drink wine and go to bed. Come on. (*Shouting*) Gertrud.

Gertrud (*off*) Yes, Herr Strindberg?

Strindberg The rest of today's rehearsals are cancelled. Call Herr Anders for ten o'clock at the Lundberg.

Gertrud (*off*) Yes, Herr Strindberg.

Strindberg Come on. I'll keep my promise to you if you'll keep yours to me. Show me brightness and goodness. Let's be at peace with other people and first of all with each other. What you need is a warm room and a good rest.

Harriet You always think you know what I need.

Strindberg I love you.

Harriet No, you think I'm a character you've written. Or a character you're still writing.

Strindberg I love you. Tell me what you want. I want you to be you.

Harriet I don't want to be your actress in life. This is the only life I've got, and it's mine. I want to write it.

Strindberg Let's go home.

Harriet No.

Strindberg What do you mean? You can't stay here.

Harriet You go to your flat. I'll go somewhere else.

Strindberg Where?

Harriet Somewhere. I'll be all right. (*She puts her coat on*)

Strindberg You're my wife. You belong in my home and my bed.
Harriet I belong to me. I'll act in your play, but I won't sleep in your bed.
Not tonight and not tomorrow.
Strindberg When?
Harriet We'll see.
Strindberg What about the baby?
Harriet If I'm pregnant, I'll have the baby. It'll be my baby. I won't give it
your name. It'll be Bosse, not Strindberg.
Strindberg You can't do that.
Harriet I think you'll find I can.

He starts to go, moving like an older man

Strindberg Where are you going to sleep tonight?
Harriet I'll be at the Lundberg in the morning.
Strindberg Are you going to sleep with another man?
Harriet No.
Strindberg I'm sorry. I could be more gentle. Please give me another
chance.
Harriet No.
Strindberg Just one more chance. Please. Please.
Harriet Not tonight.
Strindberg When?
Harriet We'll see.
Strindberg Have you no mercy? No ability to learn? I'll still be learning on
my deathbed, but you, you haven't even learnt how to keep the game alive.
A woman is like a cat with a mouse. Pounce too hard and you put an end
to your own pleasure. You aren't feeding me enough hope. I'm starving.
Harriet You'll survive.
Strindberg (*unhappily*) I'm so happy about the child. You don't know how
happy I am.
Harriet Goodbye, Gusten.

She exits

*Left alone, Strindberg goes to the table. Mumbling morosely, he scribbles a
note. Eventually we hear:*

Strindberg You think it's a comedy. It's not even a tragedy. It's a farce.

Fade to Black-out

SCENE 3

The stage has been stripped bare: the furniture, props and paraphernalia for the play have been taken away. When they rehearse, it's with whatever they used in the first act — ladders, planks, old stools and chairs from the set that was here during the fire. Floodlights have been installed at either side of the stage

Bengt enters. He paces about and looks at his watch. Harriet enters, out of breath. It doesn't look like a rehearsal

Harriet Have you been here long?
Bengt It seemed like a long time, because I knew you were with him.
Harriet I was longing to be with you.
Bengt What did you tell him?
Harriet Nothing. But he knows I'm no longer in love with him.
Bengt Don't say anything yet.
Harriet We'll have to tell him soon.
Bengt Not yet. He's going to take it badly.
Harriet I'm sure he knows already, with part of his mind.
Bengt In that case, it would be kinder to tell him.
Harriet Shall I tell him?
Bengt What would you say?
Harriet That we love each other. But it's awful to be happy when he's going to feel so much pain. I didn't choose to love you. But I'll never ...
Gertrud (*prompting from the audience*) Never forget my duties as a wife and mother.
Harriet Can we stop for a minute?
Bengt Oh no!
Harriet I want to cut that line about duties as a wife and mother.

Strindberg enters from the stalls

Strindberg Why?
Harriet It sets her up in a different way from him.
Strindberg The difference is a fact. You are a wife and mother. He's not yet a husband or father.
Harriet We mustn't imply that women are bound by marriage in a way that men aren't.
Bengt (*an outburst*) Harriet!
Harriet Yes?
Bengt Do you want this play to open on Monday? We've got three days. Three days.

Harriet I know that. I do know that.

Bengt We've made a lot of changes. A *lot*, and that's fine, but we can't go on like this. We need every second to rehearse.

Strindberg He's right.

Harriet We need all our time in the Lundberg to rehearse on the set, but since we're working here in the evenings ——

Bengt We wouldn't need to if we hadn't wasted so much time.

Harriet If you think it's wasting time to ——

Bengt All right. It's not wasting time. We're both happy with the script changes ——

Harriet We're both? Who?

Bengt Herr Strindberg and I.

Harriet What about me?

Bengt You're the one who wanted them. I'm amazed Herr Strindberg made so many, but that's fine. All I'm saying is for God's sake let's get on with it.

Strindberg I'll tell you what. We'll take a coffee break. Then after the break, Gertrud, no more script changes. You hear?

Gertrud I'm afraid I've taken the coffee to the Lundberg.

Strindberg All right, tea.

Gertrud I'm awfully sorry, everything's there.

Strindberg All right, it can't be helped. We'll have a break anyway. Five minutes.

Harriet (*to Bengt*) Give me a cigarette.

Bengt (*feeling in his pockets*) I'll get them from my dressing-room. (*He starts to leave*)

Harriet Don't bother.

Bengt I don't mind.

He exits

Strindberg Gertrud, fetch the costume designs.

Gertrud I'm sorry, Herr Strindberg. They're in the ——

Strindberg Go to the lavatory. Go away. Leave me alone with my wife.

Gertrud Oh, I'm sorry, Herr Strindberg. I didn't understand what you meant.

She exits

Strindberg Put me out of my agony. Please. I can't concentrate. Where were you last night? Were you with him?

Harriet No.

Strindberg No, you weren't with him, or no, you won't put me out of my agony?

Harriet Leave me alone. I'm not a wife here. I'm an actress, and I have plenty to think about. Don't persecute me.

Strindberg You're persecuting me. Last night at least you might have had the decency to stay away.

Harriet Your routine no longer entertains me.

Strindberg If my child is called Bosse, people will think he's illegitimate. You realize that? You want him to suffer?

Harriet Why him? We can worry about that when she's born.

Strindberg What else did she tell you?

Harriet Who?

Strindberg Siri?

Harriet Siri? Siri gave me lessons in how to drive you mad.

Strindberg Is that meant to be funny?

Harriet Of course not. Madness isn't a joke. Shall I show you what she taught me?

Bengt enters, smoking and carrying his coat

Bengt Here we are.

Harriet I think there are two of you, and only one of you is pretending to be mad. I shall talk to the other one. (*Addressing an imaginary Strindberg*) I knew it had to happen, but I wasn't expecting it so soon. It had nothing to do with me. It was the Powers.

Bengt What is this?

Harriet All those mad scenes he plays won't seem real till he's had more experience.

Bengt Have a cigarette.

Harriet No thanks.

Bengt I got them for you.

Harriet I've changed my mind. You have one, Gusten.

She takes the cigarette from Bengt's mouth and waves it in front of Strindberg, who leans back to avoid the smoke

Smoke will scare the ghosts away. Is my face getting bigger and supernaturally beautiful? Are my lovely eyes stabbing you with black lightning? Are my lips touching yours? How many times did you possess me last night?

Bengt Do you or do you not want the play to open on Monday?

Harriet (*to Bengt*) If you ever play the Captain, don't think of him as my husband. He's a refined demon. Thinks he's clever, but bullies are cowards, and when the music starts ... Gertrud, give me some music.

Gertrud enters

(*Mimicking her*) I'm sorry, Fru Strindberg, I've taken everything to the Lundberg. (*As herself*) Then I can't do my dance, can I? I can't do a death-dance without music.

Bengt Save some of your energy for the play.

Harriet I've got my second wind. What about you? How much energy have you got?

Bengt None to spare?

Harriet How about you, Gusten? Energy to spare?

Strindberg Let's do the quiet scene.

Harriet What about you, Gertrud? How's your energy level?

Gertrud Which is the quiet scene, Herr Strindberg?

Strindberg The scene where Fru Strindberg does nothing.

Harriet The one we're rehearsing. Don't you remember? When the young Strindberg says everything must be clean and beautiful and noble.

Strindberg We wouldn't make any progress with that scene tonight. (*To Bengt*) Would we?

Harriet Don't ask him.

Bengt No, we wouldn't. It's a good idea to do the quiet scene.

Harriet Very well, I'll be a good little actress and do what I'm told. As a matter of fact, there's nothing I feel more like doing than the quiet scene. Let's go.

Gertrud and Bengt position two chairs. Gertrud goes into the stalls. Harriet and Bengt sit down. A long silence. Harriet rises and begins pacing

Bengt Why don't you play something?

Harriet What do you want me to play?

Bengt Whatever you like.

Harriet I don't know anything you enjoy. (*Pause*) Why don't you smoke?

Bengt It makes me cough.

Harriet What a pity! It was your one remaining pleasure.

Bengt Pleasure? What is that?

Harriet How would I know?

Bengt What's for supper?

Harriet The remains of the stew. There's no wine. We finished it at lunch-time.

Bengt You finished it.

Harriet Was there anything in the post?

Bengt I haven't opened it yet.
Harriet (*miming picking up unopened letters from his table*) They look like bills. (*She hands them to him*)
Bengt (*miming taking out his reading glasses and having difficulty in seeing through them*) They are.
Harriet What's the matter with your eyes?
Bengt Nothing. It's these glasses.
Harriet You need stronger lenses.

Harriet prowls about the stage

How are we going to get through the evening?
Bengt The way we always do.
Harriet What's this? (*She holds out a letter*)
Bengt Nothing.
Harriet Isn't that Karl Andersen's writing?
Bengt No.
Harriet It's a Danish stamp.
Bengt I get letters from all over the world.
Harriet You wrote to Karl.
Bengt Did I?
Harriet About what happened last summer. (*Pause*) Didn't you?
Bengt I did. Yes, I did. I'm writing about a husband who's unreasonably suspicious, so I made certain enquiries. It was like a rehearsal. I was expecting to find nothing, but ... that's where you interrupt.

Pause

Gertrud (*from the stalls; when Harriet still remains silent*) I thought we'd agreed that subject was closed.
Harriet I know what the line is. If she says that, it sounds as if they really had an affair.
Bengt That's the line. Say it.
Harriet But Siri was never ——
Bengt We just agreed ——
Harriet I didn't agree.
Bengt Stop rewriting the play!
Harriet (*in tears*) Siri was never unfaithful to you. Not once.
Bengt If you destroy this production, I'll kill you.
Harriet Try an upward inflection. Maybe the line won't fall quite so flat.
Strindberg What do you want to do, Harriet?
Harriet Change the line. We don't have to say she was never unfaithful, but we shouldn't say she was when she wasn't.

Bengt Fine. We change the line, and I'll tell you what happens next. Two minutes later you say: "One more change. We can't say this. It's not fair to Siri". Soon we have to postpone the opening for a week, and at the end of a week we're still not ready, and the play never opens. Is that what you want? (*Pause*) You've given me an idea. I'm going to write a play about an actress. She cares so much about telling the truth that if she's cast as a playwright's wife, she marries the playwright by way of research. But once she knows how to play a part, she loses interest. She's ready for her next character or her next playwright. I'll tell you something. You've got more talent than I have — far more — but you'll get nowhere. Nowhere. Acting is a profession, and you're not a professional. Ten years from now, I'll be a leading man and you'll be in the audience.

Harriet Not if I have to watch you.

Strindberg That's enough. Both of you. Harriet, go away. Go to bed. Go to wherever you're intending to spend the night and sleep. Forget Siri, forget the play. Just sleep. And when you wake up, study the script as if you'd never seen it. Imagine you know nothing about any of these people. And remember that acting depends on knowing how other people feel. Remember that, and remember your dream. "Trust the voice". Every character has a distinctive voice, but so has every play — a voice that talks to the actors before they talk to the audience. You've stopped trusting the voice of this play. You've stopped listening to any voice except the one you think is Siri's, but it isn't. It's yours.

Rain starts dripping through the hole in the roof and pattering on to the stage. It continues till the end of the play

Gertrud Shall I fetch —— ?

Strindberg No, it doesn't matter. We're going to stop. Go on, Harriet. Go away. Just go.

Harriet stands motionless while he finds his attaché case, puts his hat and coat on. He looks the same as he did when we first saw him

Good night, everyone.

Bengt Herr Strindberg. Please. What are we going to do?

Strindberg Whatever you'd like to do. And Harriet. And Gertrud, you too, of course. Thank you for all the work you've done. You've worked hard, and you've done well. Good night. (*He is about to go*) Oh, I was forgetting. I'm sorry. (*He kneels down in front of Harriet to address her stomach*) Little one, wherever you sleep tonight, I wish you peaceful dreams. Good night.

Harriet moves away, leaving him on his knees. He gets up painfully and moves stiffly. He has never looked older

Bengt Herr Strindberg. Please.
Strindberg What?
Bengt Are we rehearsing tomorrow or not?
Strindberg Whatever you wish.
Bengt Harriet, do you want this play to go on?

She moves away

Let me buy you a meal.

She is about to leave

Harriet, you've got to make a decision.
Strindberg Leave her alone.

She goes

Bengt Harriet!
Gertrud (*coming on stage*) Herr Strindberg, are you all right?
Strindberg Yes, thank you, Gertrud. A little tired. How are you?
Gertrud Me? Fine. I'm sorry about the coffee. I could easily have made some and brought it in a vacuum flask. I didn't think of that.
Strindberg Don't worry about it. You go. I'll switch off the electricity.
Gertrud You're sure you'll be all right?
Strindberg Thank you, Gertrud. Yes. Good night.
Gertrud Good night, Herr Anders, Herr Strindberg.

She exits

Bengt So what's going to happen?
Strindberg What?
Bengt What are we going to do?
Strindberg It's strange. I long for cleanness and nobility and beauty and harmony, but I always write about injustice and malevolence.
Bengt Doesn't it matter to you whether the play opens on Monday?
Strindberg Whatever happens on Monday, I shall still be alive on Tuesday. Unless the Powers decide otherwise. If I live, I shall still be able to breathe, dream, watch the birds in the park. I might even be able to write. Coming?

Bengt Yes. But do you think Harriet will come to rehearsal in the morning?
Strindberg Of course. I have to put the lights out. Do you want to leave first, or do you want to stumble with me in the dark?
Bengt I'll stumble with you.
Strindberg Thank you.

He goes off

The floodlights go off, but we aren't in total darkness. A little light is filtering into the theatre from the moonlit sky. We hear a woman weeping quietly in the wings

Strindberg comes back

Bengt Did you hear that?
Strindberg What?
Bengt It sounded like a bird. What about Harriet?
Strindberg There are two Harriets, and I still have one.
Bengt Where's the other?
Strindberg Who knows.
Bengt What if she's still in the theatre? How will she get out?
Strindberg She'll find a way.

Fade to Black-out

FURNITURE AND PROPERTY LIST

ACT I
SCENE 1

On stage: Charred flats, etc.
Oil lamp on chains
Debris; damaged furniture, singed carpets, etc.
Blonde wig on wig stand
Old writing table
Singed sofa
Chairs
Lighting panel
Gramophone
Armchair
Lectern
Ladder
Vertical posts joined together with rope
Props table. *On it:* lantern, walking-stick, parasol, decanter of water, glass, towels, records, tureen and bowl, cloth for bucket, crockery, cutlery, mop-head

Off stage: Papers, letters, etc. (**Gertrud**)
Attaché case containing scripts (**Strindberg**)
Cup of coffee (**Gertrud**)
Bucket (**Gertrud**)
Parcel containing shawl (**Bengt**)
Stove (**Gertrud**)

Personal: **Strindberg**: watch
Bengt: pencil, handkerchief, cigarettes
Gertrud: glasses

SCENE 2

Strike: Bucket

Set: Ladder (move DS), drape
Life-size costume dummy in silk dress with wig
On props table: picnic basket containing rug

Off stage: Candle (**Strindberg**)

Picture of the Virgin (**Strindberg**)
Flowerpots (**Gertrud**)
Coffee (**Gertrud**)

Personal: **Bengt**: cigarettes, matches

ACT II
SCENE 1

Strike: Dummy, wig, etc.

Set: New furniture for production:
      Bench
      Chairs
      Table
      Statues
      Desk. *On it and in it:* two sweets wrapped in black paper and tinfoil, papers, notebooks, bundles of letters tied in ribbon, faded flowers, pencils, etc.
      Two lamps (practical)
      On props table: packing case, script

SCENE 2

Off stage: Travelling bag (**Harriet**)
      Coffee (x 2) (**Gertrud**)
      Blonde wig, torn envelope (**Harriet**)

Personal: **Gertrud**: watch, handbag containing mirror and powder, script
      Strindberg: pocket watch
      Harriet: handkerchief

SCENE 3

Strike: All Act II furniture
      All props and other paraphernalia

Personal: **Bengt**: watch, cigarettes, matches

LIGHTING PLOT

Practical fittings required: 2 floodlights (ACT II, SCENE 3)
Interior. The same throughout

ACT I, SCENE 1

To open: Full stage lighting; "working lights" effect on interior of a theatre on a
snowy day with some light entering from hole in roof

Cue 1   **Bengt** notices **Strindberg**   (Page 31)
            Fade to black-out

ACT I, SCENE 2

To open: Working lights effect, and candle-light from **Strindberg**'s candle

Cue 2   **Strindberg**: "I'd completely given up hope."   (Page 42)
            Fade to black-out

ACT II, SCENE 1

To open: Working lights effect

Cue 3   **Bengt**: " ... to play Mrs Soerby in *The Wild Duck.*"   (Page 51)
            Fade to black-out

ACT II, SCENE 2

To open: Working lights effect

Cue 4   **Strindberg**: "It's a farce."   (Page 65)
            Fade to black-out

ACT II, SCENE 3

To open: Floodlight effect from practical floodlights

Cue 5   **Strindberg** goes off   (Page 73)
            Floodlights go off, leaving moonlight filtering through

Cue 6   **Strindberg**: "She'll find a way."   (Page 73)
            Fade to black-out

EFFECTS PLOT

ACT I

Cue 1   **Strindberg**: "Go back."   (Page 5)
Sound of water dripping on stage through hole in roof

Cue 2   **Bengt** puts his handkerchief in the bucket   (Page 8)
Sound of water ceases

Cue 3   **Strindberg**: "And as soon as the music starts ... "   (Page 20)
*Piano music (gramophone): Saint-Saëns "Danse Macabre".
By the time* **Strindberg** *has his fit, music has stopped and
the needle scratches in the groove*

Cue 4   **Strindberg**: "Stop that machine."   (Page 21)
Scratch sound stops as Gertrud turns gramophone off

Cue 5   **Strindberg**: " ... what I've written, shall we?"   (Page 23)
Melted ice drips through roof again

Cue 6   **Gertrud**: "I'll get a cloth."   (Page 23)
Drip stops as **Gertrud** *puts cloth in bucket*

ACT II

Cue 7   **Strindberg**: "It's yours."   (Page 71)
Water drips through roof. Continue until end of play